HALITZA:

From Romania to America

written by

Millie Fain Schneir

Copyright © 2005 by Millie Fain Schneir

ISBN 0-7414-2379-0

Published by:

INFINITY
PUBLISHING.COM

1094 New De Haven Street, Suite 100
West Conshohocken, PA 19428-2713
Info@buybooksontheweb.com
www.buybooksontheweb.com
Toll-free (877) BUY BOOK
Local Phone (610) 941-9999
Fax (610) 941-9959

∞

Printed in the United States of America

Printed on Recycled Paper

Published December 2004

I dedicate this book to my dearest friend, my sister Amy. I thank her for her love and her faith in me. "You must write a book, Micky," she would say to me. Now that she is gone, I write and think of her, appreciative of her continuing support.

Rest in peace, dearest Amy. I miss you so much.

Acknowledgements

My sincere thanks to my late husband, Milton, for his support, his patience and for his wonderful gift to me, my word processor. To my dear children for the encouragement and help they extended to me. To Sally for teaching me how to use my word processor. To Judi and Jane who proofread and typed this story onto a disc. To Dianne for editing and preparing this manuscript for publication. I am so grateful to them.

To Steve and Jerry who supported me in so many ways. To my grandson, Peter, who taught me numerous things on the processor and helped me in publishing this book. Thanks to my niece Gay for her guidance, and I thank my dear sister Claire for providing me with information for this book.

I am grateful to the family members who gave me love, support and encouragement throughout the writing process including: Stan, Tina, Lucas, Ellie, Franklin, Jessica, Jennifer, Mina, Bob, Bev, Harold, Jeremy, Rebecca, David and Carrie.

Most of all, I humbly thank G-D for making it possible for me to write a book at my age.

Prologue

Halitza is a simple word that many have not heard, yet it is profound, and in this case, so important. If it weren't for this little word and its primitive ceremony, Pincas Meirowitz wouldn't have come to America with his beautiful wife and four young children. Instead, he would have stayed in Romania and had more children, eight in all, and all of them would have succumbed to Hitler's hell.

Halitza is a ceremony that must take place for the widow who is left childless and wishes to remarry. Jewish law obligates the brother-in-law to marry his brother's widow and create a family in order to perpetuate his bloodline and carry on his name. If he is married already or refuses to marry her, the ceremony of Halitza must be performed in person. As part of the ceremony, a circle consisting of the brother-in-law, the widow, and the town elders is formed. The widow removes the brother-in-law's shoe, throws it in the circle and spits on it. This is interpreted as a ritual of degradation since the brother-in-law refuses to perform his duty. Afterwards, she is free to marry whomever she pleases.

And so in 1906, Pincas uprooted his family from their life in Romania and came to America to fulfill his obligation of Halitza.

"Take your four pieces of shit and get out of my house!" she screamed. She was shaking, her arms rigid as she grasped the small kitchen table. Her eyes were two slits and her mouth was a thin line.

She glared at her mother-in-law of just a few months and shrieked, "Get out! Adolph, get them out of here."

Adolph looked at his mother and father. How sad and bewildered they looked. Three younger sisters and a brother were standing frightened and very quiet.

"Papa, Mama, please go. What can I say? She doesn't want you in her home," Adolph said in a soft but frightened tone.

"Her home?" Papa said. "I thought it was your home, too."

"What happened? What's wrong? Did we do something to hurt you? Did we say something out of line? Gut enu (*oh dear G-d*), I don't understand," Golda said in a small voice.

Adolph started to put his arms around his mother, but he caught a glimpse of Jean's face and put his arms down.

"Mama," he said, "just go. Please, for my sake, go. We'll talk another time."

Papa said, "Come Golda, come children, let's go. There's no use in staying here. Come."

They turned slowly and left the building as if in a trance. Golda was fighting back tears as they walked silently to the train, the Culver Line. Nobody said a word. Her bottom lip trembled uncontrollably. The train station was only two blocks from Adolph and Jean's apartment, but it seemed so far. She was determined to appear in control for the sake of the children. What must they be thinking about what they had just witnessed? Oy Vey, look at those troubled little faces and my poor husband.

Once on the train, Golda sat down next to her husband. What just happened? I don't understand, she thought as she was twisting her handkerchief one way and then the other way. The steady rhythm of the train calmed her down a bit.

Finally she was able to speak, "Pina," she said quietly. "Remember when Adolph was three years old? Remember when he became so ill we almost lost him? We went to the cemetery and changed his name to Altarel (*old man*) so he would have a good and long life. Do you think we are losing him again, and this time for good?"

Pina took her hand in his and said softly, "Golda, don't worry. I think it will be alright."

"Papa," said Joey, "how come you let Jean talk to you like that? If Harry was here with us, he would have stopped her."

"Sha," said Golda. "We mustn't mention this. We will not tell the family anything. It will be cleared up, I'm sure. I'm so sorry that you children were there and heard all that. Now remember, not a word."

The train stopped at Ditmas Avenue and they slowly got off. The walk to the house was short, but it seemed so long this time. When they entered their one family single standing house, they were greeted by a cheery, "Well, how is their apartment? Did they like the cake you brought? Did you have a good time, kids? Tell me about it."

Claire, the third from the oldest and the first girl, had been reading and now, as she looked at them, she could tell that something was wrong. Golda still had the package of cake in her hand. Her father seemed drawn and the children had a sad look on their faces.

"Tell me, what happened?"

Joe couldn't control himself and blurted out, "You should'a been there. You wouldn't believe it. She was yelling and screaming and Adolph was so scared. Oh, what she said."

"I told you not to say anything. Please, Chaikala, not now. We'll talk later. Let me fix something to eat. Papa and the children have not had lunch and it is late."

"Golda," said Pina, "would you mind if I went to the front room for a while? I'm not hungry. Maybe later, when you finish with the children you'll make me some demitasse. Yes?"

"Of course Pina, go rest. Poor Papa, he's all tired out." Pina went into the front room. It was a room that was used for very special company, if there was a death, G-D forbid, or maybe to discuss a wedding.

The table smelled of lemon oil and was highly polished. The lounge and the two straight-backed chairs were exactly angled on either side of the table. There was a rocker in one corner of the room with a small end table next to it. Pina sat down wearily and slowly started to rock.

What's happening to our family? Why did I come to America? Who needs this? My son, such a fine boy, so well educated, a college boy. Where do you find such a shidduch, such a match? I thought she was a good girl—pretty and a Romanian, too. We didn't want a dowry, not that they offered any. We just wanted our son to be happy and to have a fruitful life. He was already in business for himself. I remember when I gave him the money to buy that meager business.

"Papa," he said, "the window will say, **Pincas and Adolph Meirowitz**."

"No." I said. "If you are going to be open for business on the Sabbath, my name will not appear."

And so it became **Adolph Meirowitz and Brothers**. They were doing very nicely when Mr.

Abromowitz found out that there was an eligible bachelor who was handsome and well off. He promptly called in a matchmaker to arrange the meeting.

Pina was very willing for the young people to meet and the fact that the family was Romanian was a plus. Mr. Abromowitz had a pushcart and sold shoes and slippers, mostly mismatched. They were poor people, but that was no disgrace. Everything was so pleasant just a few weeks ago. Jean was a quiet girl, eager to please our son and us, and now this change.

"Oh my Golda, thank you." He took the little cup of coffee from her and took a sip. How delicious. No one could make demitasse like his Golda. "I'll stay here for a while."

"I'll be in shortly," she replied. "Drink. Rest. It's been such a mishigona day. I'll finish my kitchen and we'll go to bed." She gently stroked his head and quietly closed the door behind her.

Pina sipped the coffee and then carefully put the cup down on the table and closed his eyes; his thoughts took him back to Romania and his youth.

SOLOMON MEIROWITZ

Solomon Meirowitz always rose up early in the morning. His day started with morning prayers. He was not known for his business ability. He depended on his wife, Rachel, for all matters pertaining to money. He was a kind and gentle man who enjoyed reading from the Talmud and talking with the men who would drop in to visit or meet in the synagogue.

He washed and brushed out his beard and then put on his tallis, a white fringed prayer shawl with royal blue strips on each end. He then bound his tefillin around his arm and forehead, faced east and began his prayers. When he finished, he smiled as he returned his tallis and tefillin to the velvet bag.

Tefillin consist of two leather boxes attached to two leather straps. The boxes contain prayers and biblical passages. Starting at the age of thirteen, a Jewish man is obligated to perform the ritual of putting on tefillin. He wraps one box onto his forehead and the other onto his forearm. The Torah says, "You shall bind them as a sign upon your hand, and they should be for a reminder between your eyes."

I'm a lucky man, he thought. I have a fine wife, four children, and a home. What more could a man want? My children, two boys and two girls are all healthy, good looking, obedient children.

He looked out of the window of their modest home. The year was 1861, and it was a bleak day in this town of Derihoa, Romania. Derihoa was a small, unimpressive town, with a synagogue, a church, general store, grocery, bakery, blacksmith and barbershop. People were friendly and, for the most part, hardworking. Solomon and Rachel were happy.

It was cold and it looked like it would snow. The weather never bothered Shloma, as he was called. He was a satisfied man, grateful for what G-d had

6

given him. Pinicas was his oldest son, a fine young man, of sixteen. And then there was Meyer, getting ready for Bar Mitzvah. Ida, ten and Helen, the youngest, was six.

"Good morning, Papa." Pinicas came into his father's room. "I finished my morning prayers and I have something exciting to tell you. You'll be surprised to know that the Tolna Rabbi is coming to our village. Our Rabbi formed a posse to meet him and escort him to us. Guess what? I was invited to be part of the group to go. What do you think of that?"

"My son, you are a fine horseman. No wonder they asked you. The Tolna Rabbi is a very pious man. It is a great honor to have him in the village."

Shloma looked lovingly at his handsome son. Aye, he thought, pretty soon we'll make a match for him. He is so desirable, a well educated, pious, strong, capable, trustworthy, fine young man. Some father will be anxious to have him for a son-in-law and will be very generous.

"Go my son," he said, "G-d be with you."

The boys met at the synagogue and started to mount up.

"Pinkolie," one of them called out, "your horse needs new shoes so he will be replaced by this one. He's a bit frisky and wild, but you can handle him. I think you're the only one that can."

7

"Sure," said Pina. "We'll get along fine, won't we?" He patted the horse and mounted him easily saying, "Steady, boy, steady."

It was very cold, blustery, and starting to snow. As they proceeded to ride into a gallop, the horse was acting peculiar, bounding up and down. The snow was blinding and the horse was not easy to handle.

"Steady, boy, steady," he encouraged, but the horse would not be calmed. He threw Pina off and galloped away leaving him in a snow bank.

The boys didn't miss Pina until they reached the Rabbi. "Where is Pina?" they wondered. They found him on the way back. He was unconscious in the snow bank. When they came home, they put his frozen foot in a tub of hot water.

Gangrene set in and surgery became inevitable. His foot was amputated. The front part and the heel were round like a ball. He stayed in the hospital in Vienna for several weeks and returned home with a heavy brace.

He was strong and had a very positive attitude and pretty soon he was enjoying life with his friends, dancing with the girls, riding his horse, and being one of the boys.

"Pinkolie, will you dance with me?" the girls begged.

"Pay the klezmer and I'll dance." The musicians were called the klezmer. They played ethnic music and the young people loved to dance to it. They would throw some coins into a provided basket and the musicians would play. And so it was that Pina had a good time.

His father knew that his son was no longer the desirable match he had been before. He was what was called damaged merchandise. The elite and the rich people in the village were not interested in a man without a foot. This saddened Shloma a great deal, but he told himself it was G-d's will and it would be all right in the end.

GOLDA ABROMOWITZ

She was a beautiful little girl, born to Hyam and Yita Abromowitz, who owned a tavern in Derihoa, Romania. They had a son who was much older than Golda. He was already married and had two daughters just a little older than Golda. Yita had trouble conceiving and never thought she would become pregnant and have another child after Itzik was born. She and Hyam were surprised and delighted by their daughter and named her Golda.

Golda was a happy and healthy child and loved the animals her family raised. They had a cow, some horses, chickens ducks, a dog and a cat. She loved to feed the ducks and chickens. She was a bright girl and was eagerly waiting to learn to read and write.

Hyam made a fine living from his tavern. He sold wheat and grains to the local farmers. They often would stay over enjoying Yita's good cooking and were happy to pay for the lodging. He could easily afford to engage a teacher for his daughter. He made arrangements for a young man to come to the house to teach Golda when she turned eight years old. She was delighted and was counting the months for her birthday.

They were not close with their son Itzik. Their daughter-in-law, Toba, was very domineering and wouldn't allow him or their daughters to visit very often. To his parents' dismay, Itzik didn't cross her at all.

"Why is he so afraid of her?" Yita would ask her husband.

"I don't know," he would answer. "He sure is a weak man. I am ashamed of him. I wonder if his children respect him."

"How could they," Yita remarked. "Their mother tells them not to come here and he doesn't say a word, nothing at all. No argument, whatever she says goes. She's the boss."

Golda wanted to play with her cousins (as she called her brother's children), and she begged her mother to have them come or allow her to visit them. But Toba would not allow it.

"They are too busy with school and their friends," Toba would say to Yita whenever she invited them. "Maybe some other time." Unfortunately, that never happened.

Hyam took ill suddenly and after a short time, he passed away. It was very hard for Yita without Hyam. She tried to run the business by herself, but she couldn't. She too was getting sick and called upon her son to help her.

Itzik came with Toba, who began to run the house as well as the business. She wasn't very kind or considerate to Golda and it frightened Yita to see how harshly she spoke to her child. Golda had become sad and listless.

It was evident that Toba's girls were treated differently. They were spoken to kindly and were not expected to do anything but have fun. They were not encouraged to play with Golda or even to speak to her. That hurt Yita very much. They all lived together for about one year and then Yita died.

Toba was a mean, selfish woman. After her mother-in-law died, she and Itzik continued to take care of Golda and manage the business. Hyam and Yita had left money to be used for Golda's care and education. However, Toba had other plans for the money. She used it to clothe and educate her own daughters and turned Golda into little more than a scullery maid.

"Don't expect to live here with us and do nothing," Toba said to Golda harshly, "things are different now."

Golda was expected to do many chores, including scouring the pots. She was far too short to reach the sink, so Toba provided a box for her to stand on.

"These pots have to be clean," she barked at Golda. If they weren't Toba would strike her hands with a rolling pin, saying, "What good are you to me? You are a worthless girl. I feed you and give you a bed to sleep in and what do I get in return? Dirty pots. I wish I could get rid of you."

These were indeed hard times for Golda. She longed for the gentleness and love she had with her parents and, many a night, she cried herself to sleep. As time passed, life for Golda was meaningless. The only pleasure she had was feeding the farm animals. Whenever she had a spare moment, she would play with the dogs and the kittens. Golda rarely had enough time to look out the window at the rolling land and the calm skyline.

One day, when Golda had just finished feeding the chickens, Toba said, "Golda, go upstairs and wash your face, fix your hair, and put on a dress that your cousin gave you. A gentleman is coming with a matchmaker. Maybe they will accept you for his son. Remember, don't talk. You might spoil the shidduch."

Golda sprang up the steps. "Maybe they will like me and I will get away from this place," she prayed.

She washed quickly, brushed her black hair, put on one of the cast-off dresses and took a deep breath. Oh, I hope they like me. Should I smile? Would that be too forward? And who is the boy? Is he handsome? He couldn't be. If he were, what would he want with me?

She pinched her cheeks and bit on her lips so she would have color. Leaving this place would be heaven. She would do almost anything to leave Toba. She heard voices downstairs and her heart began to pound.

"Let us see this young lady."

Toba came to the foot of the stairs and called, "Golda, come down."

Golda came down slowly and was surprised to see a kindly looking man with a neatly combed beard, a smile on his face.

"Come here, my dear, don't be afraid," Shloma said. "I don't bite."

Golda came over shyly, her eyes shining. This man was a good person she could tell, and she knew she could love him. What about his son? Was he like his father?

She stood in front of Shloma and looked into his kind blue eyes. He smiled as he contemplated her. She was a pretty girl, he thought, a bit too thin, but never mind. She would like his tall and handsome son. Even though she had no dowry, he judged that she would be a good and dutiful wife to his son, Pincas.

"Well," he addressed Toba, "you will hear from me soon."

As soon as he left, Toba said roughly to Golda, "Don't think you are going to strut around in good clothes. Get upstairs, change, and come down quickly. There are many more chores for you to finish."

GOLDA AND PINICAS

Solomon looked at his handsome son and smiled. How good looking he was and how bright. It hurt him to see him walk with a limp, but he was grateful that he could get around as well as he did.

"You called me, Poppa?" Pinicas asked.

"Yes, my son, I want to have a talk with you. You are a fine, intelligent young man and it is time you were married. I think I have a very suitable young lady for you."

Pinicas blushed and said, "Poppa, what does she look like and will I see her before you make the arrangements?"

"Yes. She lives with her brother, his wife and two daughters in the valley. I don't think she is happy. Her parents died when she was very young. She is not educated, but I think she will make a fine wife for you."

Shlomo smiled at his son and said, "She is pretty, little, and very thin, but she'll gain weight. Pinicas, I am sure you will like her. I'll let you know when you can meet her."

Pinicas was nervous. He didn't say anything more to his father, but the next day he mounted his horse and rode to the valley. He looked down and saw the tavern. There was no one around. He sat quietly on his horse for a while. Then, he pulled the reigns and his horse picked up his front legs and neighed loudly.

Golda had been sitting in her room, looking out the window. Who is that? She had never seen anyone ride like that and handle a horse like that. The next day after she had finished her chores, she went to sit by the window and there he was again. She noticed that he was a young man and he had red hair. It was late afternoon and she remembered that was when she had seen him the day before.

I wonder who he is and why he is here. She was very curious, but didn't say a word to her sister-in-law. She would only scold her for being idle and looking out the window.

She didn't have to wonder too long, for that dear man with the white beard came again the next day to talk to Toba. He asked that his son meet Golda and then make the arrangement for the marriage.

Toba told him there was no dowry, no money, but that she would scrape together some towels and other linens, saying, "You know this girl is an orphan and penniless."

Solomon assured her that it was quite all right. If it was satisfactory with her, he would return with his son at about four o'clock when he was finished with work for the day.

"Golda, finish your chores and put on a clean dress. Comb your hair and try to look pleasant. That man is coming back with his son. If he likes you, he'll marry and I'll be able to be rid of you."

"Yes, Toba," said Golda. In her heart, she was singing, thank the good Lord; it looks like I might be leaving this place! She was so nervous she couldn't put her dress on fast enough.

When she was ready, Golda decided to stay upstairs until Toba called her. She was a bit frightened. As miserable as she was now, Golda had no idea of what she might be getting into. The old man she met was so nice, but how was his son? What if he hates her? What might happen to her?

At four o'clock Toba's loud voice came up to her. "Golda, come down."

She slowly came down the steps and when she saw the young man she recognized him as the same young man on a horse she had seen from her window. She looked down at the floor so as not to stare and also not to let them see how frightened she was.

"Ah, here you are. Do you remember me?" Solomon asked her in a kind voice. Golda nodded and tried to smile, but she couldn't because she was so nervous.

"Golda, this is my son Pinicas. Pinicas, this is Golda."

"How do you do?" he said. "I rode here on my horse one day, but no one was in sight."

Golda didn't say a word. She wanted to tell him she had seen him, but she wouldn't dare.

It was an awkward moment, but Mr. Meirowitz broke the silence and spoke to Toba, "I'll speak to my wife and she will make some preparations. You might want to do so as well."

"I can do very little," she quickly answered. "I have a family to care for."

"Very well. We will take care of everything. Good day, my dear. Come, son. Everything will be fine." He smiled at Golda, and with a slight wave to Toba, he left with Pinicas.

"Well Pinicas, what do you think?" Solomon looked at his son. The boy looked a bit uneasy.

"What can I say, Poppa? I don't know the girl. I guess it's OK. She looked so scared. I feel sorry for her."

"She is scared, poor little thing," commented Solomon. "But you will be kind to her and she will be happy. I will talk to your boss, Mr. Moses, and offer to buy his business for you. I know he wants to sell. You know the business very well and will do fine. You can pay him out monthly until you own it. So, my son, how does that sound to you?" Solomon smiled fondly at his son.

"Poppa," Pinicas said softly, "I don't know what to say. You are so wonderful to me. Are you sure you can do this?"

"Yes. Your mother and I want you to make a good life for yourself and for you to have a family. We want you to be happy."

"Thank you so much, Poppa."

And so it was exactly as Solomon said. Pina and Golda were married and started a life together. The wedding was a very simple ceremony with few guests. Rachel prepared a dinner and Toba and Itzik came with their daughters. They brought nothing, no food for the celebration and no gifts or dowry.

To Golda this man was wonderful. The fact that he wore a brace and his foot was deformed made no difference to her. When she saw it for the first time, her heart went out to him in pity, but after that she hardly was aware of it. He was not hampered by it in any way. They worked together in their clait, as a store was called. They sold grains, wheat, and groceries. Golda carried sacks of grain on her back, did everything that Pina did, and was happy.

In a few months, she was pregnant. She gave birth to a baby girl. They were so happy. Being a mother didn't stop her from doing the same work she did before the baby came. One night while she was nursing the child, she fell asleep and smothered the baby. They really never got over the tragedy.

She soon found herself pregnant again and this time they had a boy. They called him Avrom. Two and a half years later, they had another boy, Herman. When he· was two, Golda became pregnant again. When this baby was born and was a little girl, they were delighted. They named her Chaika. *(The word 'chai' means to live.)* Even though boy babies were more desirable, this child was special because of what had happened to their first baby.

They lived a happy work filled life. Golda loved her in-laws, especially her father-in-law, Shlomo. She was a good cook and loved to make soup and chicken for him. Her mother-in-law, Rachel, was always busy in the business and wasn't much of a cook or homemaker.

****

It was a shock to Pina and Golda when Shloma told them that he was leaving for America. It was 1904. "I must get Meyer out or he will be taken to the army." There was never a worry with Pincas because of his foot, but Meyer was getting to that age.

Jews were considered outsiders in this country. Pinicas, along with many Jews, understood that they were considered less important than most others. They were only tolerated, but really not desired as citizens. So many fled to other lands where they would be more welcome.

"Oh, Papa, I'm going to miss you so much," cried Golda. He was like her own father. "I will miss all of you too, but it must be done."

He planned to take Rachel, Meyer, and Ida. Helen would remain with Golda and Pina. It was a sad, tearful night when they left. They left quietly as it was necessary for them not to be seen. It was unlawful to leave to the country and imprisonment might result.

America was called the Goldina Medina, the Golden Treasure in Yiddish. However, it wasn't so wonderful for them. They were poor and lonely for the children they had left behind, but they had to do it.

They opened a little store on the east side of New York City, and they sold trimmings, laces, yard goods, and such. Rachel was in charge of the business. Shloma's day consisted of morning prayers, breakfast, a morning reading, an

19

afternoon nap, and perhaps a short time in the store. He filled his day with prayers, synagogue, and talking to friends.

Meyer and Ida adjusted to the new life. Ida was an attractive, young woman and there were young men interested in her, especially one. She liked him too, but Rachel wouldn't allow it because he was not an Orthodox Jew. She soon met Maurice, a Shomray Shabbos *(a Sabbath observer)*, who was in business with his father.

"This is the man for you, Yidsel," Rachel said to Ida. "He is an observant and responsible man. He will be a good provider for you and the children to come."

Ida and Maurice married and had two little girls, Stella and Janet. Meyer married a nice girl and so Rachael and Shloma were satisfied that the children were settled.

****

"Golda, Golda, listen to the letter I just received from America."

"Oh, Papa, how is he? How is Mama? Ida? Meyer?" She was so excited; she couldn't wait to hear about these people whom she loved so much.

"Control yourself. I'll read the letter." Pina said laughing at her. "It isn't from Mama and Papa. It's from Meyer's wife."

As he read, they learned that Meyer was dead. He committed suicide by hanging himself. There was no explanation as to why. They had been married only a short time and to everyone's knowledge they were happy. Rose, Meyer's wife, wanted them to know, so Pina could say Kaddish and sit Shiva for his brother.

Kaddish: The memorial prayer which is said for the deceased.

Shiva: The survivors are in mourning and sit Shiva. It is the week following the funeral of a biological member of a family such as a mother, father, sibling or child. The bereaved do not wear shoes nor do they leave the house. They cover all mirrors and sit on low, backless stools. It is a time for accepting comfort from caring friends and family and for prayer. It is a time for remembering and adjusting to the loss. Once the Shiva week has ended, the mourners take a circular walk outside to acknowledge that life continues.

Pina and Golda both cried. "Poor Mama and Papa."

Golda said sadly, "To lose a child is the worst thing that could happen to a parent. We know that feeling, don't we, Pina?"

"Yes, Golda, we do. I will write a letter tonight and try to comfort them."

Pina and Golda now had four children and a good business. They enjoyed their simple, hard-working life and their children.

Avrom was a quiet boy. When he was a baby, he became very ill with an abscess and they almost lost him. He had a raging fever. Golda and Pina had feared for his life. They gave him a new name, Alta, which means old, hoping that he would live to be an old man. Adolph finally recovered but was a bit fragile.

Herman, on the other hand, was into everything. Small for his age, he prided himself on his strength and ability. Chaika, a beautiful child, was very bright. She learned quickly and was a joy to her mother and father. The fourth child was Hennoch. He was a darling baby of fourteen months.

Soon, another letter came from Meyer's widow Rose. This time, she told them of her desire to remarry and needed Pina to come to America to perform the ceremony of Halitza. He must perform the ceremony in person.

Being a very observant Jew, Pina consented to make the trip to America. He had planned to go alone, leaving Golda and the children home. He would return as soon as he could.

Golda refused to let him go alone. She asked, "Pina, why do you have to do this in person?"

"Golda, it is my responsibility to care for my sister-in-law," he answered. "The ceremony will release me of further obligation to her. So, I have to go."

"If you go, we all go. I can't stay here without you."

Pina looked at his wife. She was beautiful. Bearing children had rounded out her figure. Oh, how he loved her.

"Well, if we all go, then we'll stay in America," he said.

And so it was. They sent a letter to Solomon and Rachel telling them of their plans and started to prepare for the big move. It was now 1910.

MOVING TO AMERICA

The business was easily sold and for a fair price. They didn't have many valuable possessions, so the packing wasn't too difficult. Golda's beautiful heavy brass candlesticks, Pina's silver wine goblet, the samovar, a pair of plates with beautiful birds painted on them, a dozen demitasse cups, and some pictures that were important to her were all carefully packed.

There was a great deal of excitement in the village. Pincas Meirowitz was taking his family to America. Pinicas was considered a wealthy man. He had a little more than a thousand dollars in cash. That was a goodly sum in those days. He prided himself that he didn't owe anyone a cent. He was leaving during the day, free and easy, leaving with a good name and many friends.

The voyage was uneventful. The ship was crowded and uncomfortable. The food was not plentiful and not prepared the way Golda had done so at home, but they managed.

Avrom was a bit fearful, staying close to Golda as much as he could. Herman was always getting into some trouble. Golda was constantly pulling him away from some danger. Chaika was very inquisitive talking to the passengers and was very excited to be going on this adventure. Hennoch

took the trip well. He was still being breastfed by Golda and was very content.

As the ship was coming into the harbor, everyone was on deck. There was a sense of joy, fear, and excitement all around. This new land, the Goldina Medina, the land of opportunity, what would it be like?

How would it be for Pina and his family? What did it hold for them? Pina thought how wonderful it would be to see his parents and his sister again, but would it indeed hold a much better life for his wife and children? A better life than what he left behind? He stroked the top of his daughter's head and stared out into the distance consumed by these thoughts.

Finally, it was time for processing Pinicas' papers. The names of the family were changed, all except Golda. Pinicas became Pincas, Avrum became Adolph, Herman was called Harry, Chaika turned into Claire, and Hennoch was now Henry.

As they disembarked, there were people waiting. They had heard that Pincas Meirowitz was a man of means and they wanted to offer him partnerships in their businesses. There was a hardware store merchant, the owner of a milk company, and some other people. Pincas was impressed and listened respectfully.

"Thank you for asking me to join your business," he would say. "I'll think about it and let you know."

He had to consult with his father and mother and then he had to meet with Rose and take care of Halitza before he ventured into any business. To his dismay, he found his parents' business was in terrible shape. In fact, they were very near bankruptcy.

"Pina, what do you think we should do?" they asked in desperation.

"Don't worry Mama, Papa. I'll clear your name. I'll take care of all your debts," Pina said.

He tried to sound cheerful and confident, but he was so very disappointed as he saw all his dreams for good business opportunities fade away. Clearing the good name of Meirowitz took almost all of his money. He was a good and loving son and felt this was the right and only thing to do.

Pincas had to fulfill his next responsibility of Halitza with Rose. He contacted his sister-in-law and made an appointment to meet with her to plan the ceremony. Pincas found her apartment house without any trouble. She lived close to his parents. It was an old building and he walked up three flights of steps and knocked on the door. Although he knew what he would be required to do, he was a bit apprehensive because he had never see Halitza performed.

Pincas had seen pictures of Rose, which had been sent from America, so he recognized her when she opened the door. However, he was pleasantly surprised to find her so gracious, soft spoken, and well dressed. He immediately felt a sense of warmth as a brother-in-law upon meeting her. In person she was a good-looking, slender woman of medium height with short brown hair, hazel eyes, a fair complexion and a shy ready smile.

"Pinicas, I recognize you from the pictures. How was your trip? How is your family? Oh, I'm sorry you are standing in the doorway, please come in."

"Hello, Rose," he said kindly. " I'm fine and so is my family. I am so glad that I am here. I am here to get this Halitza business over with. But, Rose, if it isn't too painful, could you tell me what happened to Meyer?"

"Please sit down," she said nervously, "may I bring you a drink, a cup of coffee?"

"A glass of water would be fine, thank you."

When she left the room, he looked around. The apartment was very sparsely furnished but spotless. The couch was frayed and the table and chairs, though they were polished, were old and scratched. It was a poor person's apartment, no doubt about it.

Rose returned with the water and sat down. "I'll tell you, it is difficult for me. I think about it a lot, feeling guilty, thinking that if I hadn't left the apartment that day, he wouldn't have done it. You see, he was very depressed, he wasn't working, and he couldn't find a job."

She stopped, took a breath and continued, "He was ashamed to tell his parents and too proud to ask for help from his sister Helen. He warned me not to say anything and he wouldn't let me look for a job."

"Well, that morning," Rose continued softly, "I decided to go out and look for work. I wasn't trained to do office work, but I could have worked as a waitress or a housekeeper. I didn't care as long as we would be able to manage until he found work. When I returned, he was dead. He had hung himself. It was awful."

Rose began to cry. Although Pincas wanted to know what happened, he felt regretful that he had upset her.

"How sad," Pincas said quietly, "poor Meyer. I am so sorry Rose. You were a good wife trying to help. Please Rose, don't cry, it wasn't your fault."

"Oh Pinicas, I know your Mother and Father blame me. They refused to talk about it to me and never let me explain. I can understand their grief and bitterness, but it is very hurtful for them to treat me that way."

"Rose, I am very sorry," Pincas said. "Now, please tell me about the man you are going to marry."

"His name is Joe. He is a very nice man with two lovely, well-mannered children—a ten-year-old girl and a little boy of six. His wife was very ill and passed away. Joe really needs someone to care for him and the children. He is lonely and so am I, so we hope it will work out."

Pincas felt sorry for Rose. It surely was not a romantic situation, rather it seemed to be a practical plan for both of them.

He said, "I wish you both good luck and happiness. And Rose, I hope that you will come to our home and meet my wife and our children. You are so welcome."

"Thank you, Pinicas, I would love that," she answered.

"I have to ask you how much money you want for the Halitza?" continued Pincas.

"Joe said he would pay for me," Rose replied.

"Money for me?" Pincas questioned. "What kind of nonsense is that? I will not take any money. Can we do it tomorrow and then you and Joe can get on with your life."

"Thank you so much. Tomorrow will be fine at about one o'clock. Thank you again." Rose said gently.

The next day, Pincas arrived promptly at one o'clock. He met Joe, and the three of them silently walked to the rabbi's study in a small nearby shul.

The rabbi seemed glad to see them and greeted them, "Come in, come in. I know why you are here. Shall we get started?"

"You understand," the rabbi said to Pincas, "that if you were a single man, you would be obligated to marry Rose and have a child so as to carry on your family name. Since you are married and have a family of you own, you are asked to release Rose and make it possible for her to marry a man of her choice."

"Rose," the rabbi now addressed her, "remove you brother-in-law's shoe and throw it down. You are supposed to spit in his face because he rejected you, and then you will be released so that you can marry whomever you wish. However, we ask you to spit on the shoe instead."

The rabbi read a declaration of absolution of Pincas' obligations, and then asked Rose to compensate Pincas if she had not already done so.

Pincas spoke up quickly, "There is no compensation, no money, I'm sorry my brother is gone, but I'm glad to do what is required of me."

"Thank you again, Pinicas. I hope I will see you again and that some day I will meet your family," said Rose.

"You will see my family, and Rose, please call me Pincas. We are in America, and at Ellis Island they gave me an American name," Pincas laughed.

"Good-bye, Rose, and good luck," he said as he left.

****

Pincas worked hard in his parents' business, and they struggled greatly.

"Golda," Pina said, "we will have to get along on very little. Will you be able to manage on fifty cents a day? That is all we can afford."

"Pina, we will get along and do the best we can," Golda said. "We'll eat beans and noodles and lots of good things."

Pina looked lovingly at his wife. She was so dear and capable. They had a barter arrangement with a grocer. She traded cooked foods for staples, which included flour, sugar, coffee, tea and eggs. The fifty cents was used for milk and bread. Golda made sure that her children, husband, and in-laws were well fed.

On Friday, she received two dollars from the business for a chicken and fish for the Shabbos meal. Golda was an excellent cook and baker. The flat became a beautiful home on Shabbos. A white tablecloth, homemade challah covered with a Madeira napkin, individual bilkalach *(braided rolls)* for each child, a decanter of wine, and a beautiful goblet for the traditional Kiddush graced the table. The Shabbos candles were lit and glowed giving the home a warm, contented feeling. Pincas chanted the blessing over the wine and the goblet was passed around for all to have a sip.

"Golda, this meal is just delicious. I'm so lucky with you as my wife and our children." Pina was a proud and happy man.

****

"Pina, we are in America two years already," Golda reflected as she mended socks, "our next child will be American born." She continued thoughtfully, "Adolph is doing so well in school, he skipped a grade. Soon he will be in class with the children his own age. I wish he had a little of Herman's spirit though and Herman had a bit of

Avrom's gentleness. I do worry about Avrom. He is so afraid of everything."

"Don't worry about him so, Golda. He's a good boy. He'll be fine." Pina tried to reassure her. He had been reading *The Jewish Forward*, the Yiddish newspaper.

"Listen to this!" his voice was full of amazement. "A beggar was going through the garbage and found a newborn baby! Can you imagine anyone throwing away a child? Can you imagine such a thing?"

"Oh Pina! How horrible. I wish I had found the baby. I would keep it safe and raise it as my own. How could..." she drifted off to her own thoughts.

Pina would read the paper to her in the evening when she was through with her work. She was never taught to read and truly loved this time of the evening. She would sit and knit or mend and Pina would read her the news of the day.

"You know Golda, in two more years I'll be an American citizen. This is such a wonderful country: The Goldina Medina to be sure, no pogroms. If a man is ambitious, he can do anything. It doesn't matter if he is Jew or Gentile. It is so wonderful. All I pray is that when our children are ready to marry, they find good Romanian mates. G-d please spare us from tailors or Galitzianas."

Pincas was a bit prejudiced as were all the people in the various villages. In Europe the tailor was not considered so desirable. He was usually uneducated and poor. The Glitizianas were stingy and selfish. He thought Romanians were the most desirable. But others called Romanians gypsies and horse thieves.

"Pina! We have plenty of time to worry about that," Golda smiled and shook her head.

"I'm worried about Ida," Pina said. "Maurice is not so good to her. She gave him two nice girls and tries so hard to make him happy. He's mean to her. You know he hits her? I don't like him at all. And Helen, she should make a good marriage. Where do you find a beautiful girl, who is educated, already a schoolteacher? Alla mallas *(all good qualities)* she has. Those are things to worry about."

"Mama will find someone for Helen. Like you said, she is beautiful and I know there have been some eligible suitors recommended. Come. It's late. Let's go to bed."

Weeks later, Ida rushed into Golda's kitchen. "Golda," she was weeping. "My husband has left me and our little girls. Oh what will happen to us? How will I get along? " she sobbed.

Golda said sternly, "I never did like that man." She put her arms around her sister-in-law. "You'll manage and we'll all help. Where did he go?" They sat quietly for a moment.

Ida was a bit more composed now. She sighed and shook her head. "I don't know where he went, but I'll find out from his mother. I know she likes me and I really like her. If she knows, she will tell me."

"OK. Sit down over here Ida," Golda said as she pointed to a kitchen chair. "I'll make a mamiliga and coffee for you and you soon will be feeling better."

She was famous for her mamiliga, a dish made from yellow corn meal. The trick is to cook it so that when it is done, it comes out like a soufflé. Mama cut it with a thread and served it to Ida with brinza, similar to pot cheese. It is stronger tasting with a larger curd than pot cheese.

Ida smiled and looked at Golda lovingly. "No one makes mamaliga like you."

"Thank you, dear Ida. Now, you must do something about your situation. Maurice is your husband and the father of your girls. He has to be responsible and support them and you. I do hope your mother-in-law knows where he is."

Poor Ida, she has no mazel, thought Golda as she cleared the table. Ida had gone to see her mother-in-law. What would I do if Pina ever left me? G-d forbid. Oh, I can't bear to think such a thing. I was smart not to let him go to America without the children and me. I heard about men who left for America and really planned to return home or send for their families, but never did. Some started a new family. Oy vey, what could happen in this world!

She washed and dried the dishes, picked up her basket of mending and sat down on her favorite chair by the window. She could see what was going on in the street, see her children coming home. She smiled. How lucky I am, she thought.

We have six children and one on the way, all healthy and beautiful.

It was getting a bit harder for Pina to get around. The brace was beginning to feel heavy and he used a cane to help himself walk. Poor man, he suffered a lot and never complained. But he was happy and so proud of his growing family.

"Golda," he would say, "do you know why our children have such beautiful eyes? Not one wears glasses. That's because I lead a clean life. I have never fooled around with other women or anything, even when you were not well."

Golda heard the clock chime. I'd better hurry, she thought. I must get supper ready. She put her mending into the basket and went into the kitchen.

RACHEL MEIROWITZ

Rachel Meirowitz rose early, washed, dressed, said her morning prayers, and planned her busy day. She had to serve Shloma his breakfast, go to the store to work with her son, Pina and then sell some theater tickets for the Jewish show. She would go to her friends and neighbors and would not leave until they bought from her. Her new founded charity needed money and the Jewish shows were profitable.

The organization was called "Rachel Mierowitz Kimpitoren Fahrine" (*Rachel Meirowitz' New Mothers Organization*). She started it in order to help young families make ends meet. Rachel would provide these poor women with a small layette of little flannel gowns, some diapers, a chicken, carrots, onions, potatoes, and other necessities. She sewed the little garments with some women.

When her granddaughter Chaika, now called Claire, was eight years old, she taught her to sew and she joined the group. The organization grew and had many members. In time, they were able to provide more and more for the needy.

"Golda, don't give the children such large portions of soup and meat. They don't really need all that. Give me the leftovers and I'll serve them at the Lava Malka (*celebration at the end of the Sabbath*) to the poor men on Saturday evening after Havdalah (*the Saturday night ceremony that marks the end of the Sabbath*). She would look for every opportunity to provide for those in need.

As time went on, her organization grew even larger and women would come from quite a distance to join in the work. Rachel worked hard to raise money. Every penny she could spare went into this project. As a result, she neglected to attend to some of her own needs.

"Mama, your mouth looks so bad. You need teeth," Helen said as she had several times before. Rachel had very few teeth and as a result, could not chew very well. "I will send you some money."

"Oh Helen dear, thank you. You are such a good daughter. May G-d bless you."

"Never mind that Mama, just be sure you do it this time." Helen had given her money for her teeth before, but Rachel would use it for bolts of cloth for the layettes and for food for the needy.

"I'll do it this time. We had the opportunity to buy goods so inexpensively. I just couldn't refuse. You understand, don't you dear?"

"Yes Mama, I understand. But please, this time go to the dentist and get it done."

Helen had married Moses Asher. He was in silks and velvets and was a very wealthy man. She didn't love him when they first married. In fact, she didn't want him for her husband. But Rachel liked him and was sure he would be a good provider for her daughter.

Love would come. Moe, as he was known, was shorter than Helen and not as well educated. But he adored her and wanted to do anything to make her happy. In turn, Helen introduced him to a life of culture. He became acquainted with good literature, plays, and fine music.

They were happy and Helen became very devoted to him. She had a deep respect for him and was careful to never let anyone think that she knew more than he. When she was asked a question, she would always answer, "I'll ask Moe". They had three children who were educated at Ethical Culture, a private school, and they enjoyed a fine life.

1913

Golda was in bed after having just given birth to a baby girl, her seventh child. She had eleven pregnancies, one miscarriage, and one child who died while she was still living in Europe.

"What a beautiful child," she said proudly. "We will name her Libba Rifka."

When the midwife had finished her work, she began to fill out the birth certificate. "What is the baby's name?" she asked.

Claire, who had been reading *Little Women* at the time, quickly and firmly said, "Her name is Amy Rebecca."

"What kind of name is that?" the midwife asked.

"My mother said her name will be 'Libba Rifka' in Jewish and that's Amy Rebecca in English," Claire replied smartly.

****

"Where are the years flying and so fast?" exclaimed Golda as she looked at her handsome family. "Everyone is getting so old."

Adolph was going to college to learn business. He went at night so that he could work for his Uncle Moe during the day. Poor Adolph, she thought as she brought him a shiny, red apple to help him stay awake. "My son, you work so hard, both day and night."

"It will be worth it, Mom. When I become rich, we'll all take it easy." It hurt him to see his family struggling. Some day all of them will have everything they want, he thought. I'll see to it.

He attacked his books with new vigor. Golda kissed the top of his head and warned him not to stay up too late. She wanted him to stay healthy.

She closed the door quietly and went into the bedroom where Pina was getting ready for bed. He removed the brace on his foot. Oh, what a relief. It was getting harder and harder to carry it.

He had consulted an orthopedic doctor who suggested that the foot be amputated and a special shoe without a brace be worn. The doctor tried to convince Pina that such a shoe would enable him to do much more and he would be able to enjoy life. Pina chose not to have the operation because of the expense and the long time he would need to recuperate. He lived to regret that decision.

"Pina, that boy works so hard. I worry. He's not strong," Golda said as she entered the room.

"Golda dear, don't worry. He'll be fine. I just know it. He's very bright. I think soon we'll be able to put him in a business like Moe's. He's teaching Adolph and Harry a lot about silks and velvets. He is a fine man, that Moe."

"Yes he is. Helen is very happy with him. She has made such a fine gentleman out of him." Golda smiled.

Then she looked concerned, "Oh Pina, I didn't mean that he wasn't a fine man before. It's just that he has become so educated. It's really wonderful that he and Helen can share so much."

"Well she wanted her marriage to be a solid, happy one. She loves music, books, and culture and so she taught him. He also seems to enjoy those things. Good for her. But enough talking," he said softly. "Come to bed."

****

"Mama," said Claire, "I'm going to let Leah take a bath in our tub. Okay?"

Golda disliked friction in the house and tried to avoid problems. "You know that Harry doesn't want anyone in the tub except our family. So why look for trouble." She was hoping that Claire would sense her uneasiness.

"I'll let her come when he's not home." Claire was insistent.

Leah was her close friend as were Dinah and Sophie. They called themselves the four musketeers. These girls were loyal to each other, best friends. They went everywhere together. When they decided to go to the movies, they all knew that Claire's little sister had to come along.

"You cannot go unless you take Nettie with you," Golda said. Nettie was Golda's fifth child, her first child born in America.

"She's such a pest. She never likes the seat she is sitting in and always wants to change it. Then, after a while, she wants to go home. Gosh, Mom, do I have to take her? My friends don't like it either." Claire was almost in tears.

Golda looked at the little pinched face of her daughter. It was so earnest and so pleading. "Chaikala, mine kind (*my child*), you cannot leave your sister. She has nothing to do and she loves to be with you. So take her. I'll tell her to behave."

"Leah," Claire said as they were walking to the movies, "I asked my mother about you coming over for a bath. She said it was fine with her, but you know my brother, Harry. So if you come when he's not home, it will be good. Okay?"

"Yes," answered Leah excitedly, "you are so lucky to have a bathtub in your house. Thanks. Is tomorrow after school all right?"

"Yes, we just have to make sure that Harry is not home," said Claire. Harry made deliveries for Uncle Moe after school and usually returned home about six o'clock in the evening.

Leah came timidly to the door the next afternoon. "Is it okay, Claire?" she asked.

"Yes, yes, come in. Hurry up. He won't be home until six."

They prepared the tub, filling the bucket with water from the sink and pouring it into the tub.

"There, that's enough. Get in," said Claire. "Isn't it great?"

Golda smiled as she looked and listened to her daughter while she began the preparations for supper. It was nice to see the pleasure Claire was having making her friend happy. Oy vey, she thought. I hope Harry is a little late tonight. I

40

shudder to think how he would act if he found Leah here and in the tub.

Claire was nervously watching out the window for fear of Harry returning, and sure enough, there he was coming down the street. "Leah, hurry, you have to leave. Harry is coming. Oh, get out of the tub quickly. You have to go."

Poor Leah. She grabbed her towel and put her under things on her wet body. Her skirt and blouse unbuttoned, she quickly climbed out of the window onto the fire escape and down to the street just as Harry entered the house.

"Hello, Mom. How's everything? You okay?"

"Yes, Hershila, everything is fine. Soon we'll eat."

"What are you doing, Claire?" Harry asked suspiciously.

"I'm just emptying the tub for next time," she answered, trying to act calmly while not mentioning Leah. The incident passed and Claire sighed with great relief.

****

America was at war. Pincas read *The Jewish Forward* as well as *The New York Post* to Golda and they were both very concerned. They loved this free country and were proud to be American citizens. They learned about the candidates, their platforms, and gave their decision much thought before casting their votes. They took the privilege of voting very seriously.

"Pina," Golda asked, "do you think they will draft our Alteral? He's so fragile, so gentle. Oh, I'm so scared."

Pina put his arm around her and said, "He is no different from any other boy, but maybe the war will be over before he becomes of age. G-d will take care of our country and our sons."

When Claire noticed her mother's swelling stomach, she became furious. "Are you pregnant again? How disgusting!" She was almost crying.

"Chaikela, Chaikela, don't be upset. It's a blessing. You'll realize it when you grow up."

"I know how children are born. I read about it, and I told the girls just how it happens. Gosh, you and Papa are old, too old to have another child!" Claire was angrily pushing tears away from her cheeks. "What am I going to tell my friends?"

Now it was Golda who became annoyed. "Claire, stop this right now. I think you read too much. There is nothing shameful about having a child. It is beautiful, and we'll talk no more about it.'"

The boys in the area were being drafted for the Army, Navy, and Marines. Adolph went for the mail and found his orders to come to the recruiting office.

"Adolph, what's the matter?" Golda looked at his pale face and became alarmed. "You look so upset. Tell me what's in that letter?"

"I'm drafted. Oh, I knew it would happen, but I didn't think I would feel this way. I'm scared."

Pina had just walked into the kitchen and overheard most of the conversation. "Adolph," he said, "it certainly isn't the best news, but we are Americans, and our country needs our help." He felt so sad himself, but what could he or anyone do? His son wasn't the only boy drafted.

"With G-d's help, you'll do fine," he said.

He noticed Golda twisting the kitchen towel and he could tell she was upset. She had that habit. When she was worried or hurt, she would twist and untwist whatever she had in her hand.

"Golda, don't worry. We don't even know if he'll be taken and for what. They may not want him, or maybe they'll give him an office job. Please, Goldila, don't worry. Have faith. Everything will turn out all right with G-d's help."

Adolph said nothing, but looked hopefully at his father.

Harry was listening and he jumped from his chair and put his arm around his brother. "I'll go for you, Adolph. I'll win the war! I'll go down to the recruiting station and take care of it. You won't have to go."

He dressed carefully so as to make a good impression and rode his bicycle to the station.

"Listen," he said, "you called my brother and he's chicken. He's a great guy, but he's weak and scared. Take me instead. I'm strong and I'll win the war for you."

"Get lost, kid," said the officer. "Beat it!" Harry persisted and was escorted out the front door.

A few minutes later he came in through the back entrance and said, "You're making a big mistake. Take me!"

The officer was annoyed and he grabbed Harry by the collar and said in a rough manner, "Listen kid, listen to me. I thought I told you to beat it. You are too young and we do not want you. Now get going." He shoved Harry out the door.

The family was very involved with the progress of the war and very concerned with Adolph's attitude. He was sad and seemed so nervous. The whole family moved about in a quiet manner.

Harry would always say, "I can't understand why they wouldn't take me instead of Adolph. I really want to go and I would be a darn good soldier."

Adolph filed the papers, did everything he was supposed to and was waiting for his orders. To his and everyone else's joy, the war was over and America was victorious.

****

It was the fourth of July, 1917. The boys went to Coney Island to see the fireworks. Claire and Nettie were dancing in the street to the music of the organ grinder and little Amy was watching.

"Pina, I think it's time. Better get the midwife," said Golda.

"Right away." He opened the door and called, "Claire, go to the midwife and tell her to come."

"I'm dancing, I'll go later."

"You'll go now, right now, and hurry up," said Pina firmly. Claire went and it didn't take long for Golda to give birth. It was a girl and they called her Malka.

When the boys returned home from Coney Island they found they had a new little sister. Adolph picked her up and danced with her. Golda smiled and thought he could be her father and what a wonderful husband and father he'd make some day.

The family settled in and everyone was busy. Some were in school and some were working, but all were helpful in some way in the home.

Nettie, young as she was, watched her mother cook and bake and was so proud when she could help. She was very clean about herself and in the house. She was showing signs of becoming a real beauty with blond hair, large blue eyes, full mouth and a gentle smile.

"When I get married, I'm going to cook and bake just like you, Mama," she said.

"Oh, momala," Golda answered as she hugged her daughter. "You'll be a better cook and homemaker than I, but thank you for saying that."

BROOKLYN

Pincas came into the kitchen and sat down wearily. "This brace is getting heavy," he said. "Golda, what would you say if I told you we were moving to Brooklyn, near 13th Avenue? I found an apartment. It's nice and big. I didn't tell the landlord how many children we had. He didn't ask. All I said was that our children were quiet and well behaved. He said okay. I then said, If it's all right with you, we can move in next month."

"What about Mama and Papa? Can we leave them?" Golda was concerned.

"They will be fine," Pina said. "We'll visit them every week, on Saturday evening after Havdalah. They are going to sell the store soon so they won't need me. I think it will be a good move. Brooklyn is beautiful, Golda, grass, trees, some real big houses. Someday, we'll have a house. It will be so good for the children."

The day they moved, all the children didn't come at once. Golda and Pincas brought the baby, Amy, Joey, and Nettie. The others came in quietly at night.

Golda loved to shop on 13th Avenue. "Such stores," she would say. "I would have bought more, but I couldn't carry anymore." She had a large black shopping bag and it was filled to the brim when she came home.

It was a bit crowded in the apartment and even though the landlord didn't say anything or complain to the children or for that matter to Golda or Pincas about noise, the family was uncomfortable. Pina began to hunt for a house. He found a freestanding wooden house with four bedrooms, bath, front room, dining room, nice kitchen, and a backyard.

"This is a good house for us," Pina told Golda when he returned from his walk. "It's not far from the shul. I can easily walk it, and we will be able to build a sukkah (*a hut with a partially open roof built for use during the holiday of Sukkot*). I think that we'll be very happy."

Golda was so excited. "Pina, can we afford a house? It will be so wonderful. I can't believe it. There will be plenty of room and a yard, too. I'll plant flowers and a rosebush. Oh, how I love roses! We'll plant vegetables, too. Tomatoes are so delicious when they are homegrown. Pina, it's a dream come true. You are such a good husband and father," she said. "I'm a lucky woman."

"Aye, Goldala, it is I who is the lucky one," said Pincas. "I thank the good Lord for my blessings. A good wife, fine children, and all are healthy. Not one needs eyeglasses. Tomorrow I'll take you over to the house. You'll see if you like it. I think you will."

"I know I will. I know I won't sleep a bit tonight. I'm so excited."

The house was a delight to Golda and the family. Harry planted a rosebush on the front lawn. The boys washed the windows, mowed the lawn, and did all the outside work. They dug up a bit of the backyard for Golda's vegetables. The girls helped her in the house. They were so happy.

To the delight of Pincas and Golda, Solomon and Rachael visited them often. They had sold the store upon the insistence of their daughter, Helen.

"Mama, Papa, please sell that store. What do you need it for? Moe and I want to help you move into a nice neighborhood. We can afford it and we want you to be happy," said Helen earnestly.

Rachael looked at her daughter and smiled. "We really appreciate and love you for caring, but it is fine here. We don't need to move to a better neighborhood. It's where we want to live," said Rachael.

"Don't worry about us, Helen. You and Moe are so good and generous to us. Your father and I are very happy here with our friends, the shul my organization. Oh, I couldn't leave." She bent over and kissed her daughter.

"All right, all right, stay dear Mama, but Moe and I want to take care of you and all your expenses. We want you to get rid of the store," pleaded Helen.

Moe Asher became a millionaire in the yard goods business. He was a very ambitious man and bought oil wells in Louisiana. He became even richer. They were very happy with their three children, two girls and a boy.

****

Golda sat down on her favorite rocker on the porch. It was a beautiful afternoon in the early summer. She picked up her almost finished afghan and began to knit and rock slowly. I can't sit too long because I have to prepare the beets and baked potato for Claire when she comes home from work.

Golda smiled when she thought about her oldest daughter. She had a very good job, brought home her salary, and took very little for herself, just enough to cover her traveling and lunch expenses. Claire was fifteen when she applied for a job as a typist. She was offered $10 a week, but she refused saying that she needed more money and if they would give her a chance, she would prove her worth. She was given $12 and was so well liked that she was given many raises from time to time.

Oy vey, thought Golda. Claire has a pisk *(mouth)*, G-d bless her. She's teaching me to cook healthy foods like little whole beets cooked with the skin so as not to kill the vitamins and baked potatoes, very well scrubbed so one could eat the skin. Oh well, I'm doing it for her, she's a good girl, hard working and so bright.

Claire had many chances to marry wealthy men. They would take her to fine places like the Moulin Rouge, bring her flowers and candy, but she liked Alex. They met at the Infant's Home, an organization that supported orphans. Alex was president and Claire worked hard there. I don't blame her for liking him; he's a dear boy, nebech, poor thing, an orphan. He's so good. Oh, I must get started; she quickly put her knitting into her basket and went into the kitchen to prepare dinner.

****

Nettie was a beautiful girl, long blond hair, a slender well-shaped body and a sweet, gentle manner. Golda was allowing her to go to the beach with some girls.

"Be careful, momala," Golda said. "Don't go out too far in the ocean, and be sure there is a lifeguard, and don't talk to strangers."

"Oh Mama, don't worry, I can take care of myself, and Mama, thank you for this beautiful bathing suit, I love it," answered Nettie, as she kissed her mother.

"Oy, you look so good in it. I'm a little worried," said Golda as she returned the embrace warmly and smiled at her daughter. "Have a good time and go safely."

Nettie was walking along the water's edge and was indeed a beautiful sight. The one piece black bathing suit fit her perfectly, her long blond hair glistened in the sunlight, her blue eyes were bright and the pleasure she was experiencing walking in the cool water was evident on her smiling face.

"Oh Ruthie, we are so lucky to be here. I love the beach, it's so cool, I could stay here forever," she said.

Ruth Gordon was Nettie's friend and they went everywhere together. She didn't rely on Claire to go to the movies anymore; she had her own friends, especially Ruthie.

"Excuse me, may I speak to you for a minute or two?" Nettie and Ruth looked at a very handsome Chinese man who was dressed neatly and had a tripod camera that he had planted in the sand. He smiled and told them that he was a photographer and would be very honored if the young lady in the black suit would pose for him.

"I work for a company that makes calendars, and I think your picture on one would make my boss very happy, and that would be good for me." He spoke so sincerely and Nettie felt flattered, surprised, and a bit perplexed.

"What should I do, Ruthie?" Ruth look concerned.

"I don't know," she said. "What will your mother say? I really don't know."

The man smiled and said, "Don't be afraid. I'll bring the picture to your home."

Nettie finally agreed and posed for him.

"Thank you," he said. "Where do you live?" Nettie told him and the two girls continued to walk.

"Did you have a good time?" Golda looked up from her mending.

"Oh, yes, Mama," she answered excitedly. "A man took my picture and he's going to put it on a Chinese calendar, and he's going to come here and give me a picture."

"What?" exclaimed Golda. "You gave a man your address? Are you meshuga? Oh, my dear Lord, what made you do a thing like that?"

Nettie looked at her mother and said softly, "Mom, he was so nice and polite. Oh, Mom, I'm so sorry I made you angry."

"I'm not angry, momala. I'm worried, and yes, I am angry, but at myself, not you. I should have told you never to give your address or phone number or even talk to strangers," Golda said sadly.

"I'll never do that again, Mama," Nettie replied as she put her arms around her mother. 'Don't worry, Mom. Please don't, it'll be okay."

"I hope so, but remember, in the future, do not give out information about yourself, where you live, what you do, just don't talk to boys or men you don't know." Golda picked up her knitting, made a few stitches, and put it down with a thud. "I have to get supper ready," she said aloud, and went into the kitchen.

On a hot summer morning the following week, Golda had swept the walk, watered her rosebush, and was hosing down the sidewalk, when she saw a young Chinese man coming up toward her.

"Excuse me," he said, "are you Mrs. Meirowitz?" When she nodded her head, he smiled and continued to speak.

"Good morning, I'm Alfred Tang, and may I say your roses are just beautiful. Do you feed the soil?"

Golda was very proud of her roses and was pleased at his admiration for them, but she was uneasy with this stranger. He was a medium height, handsome man with a ready smile and was holding a large box covered with a flowered cloth.

"Yes, I do, feed the earth, that is. What brings you to my home?"

"You have a beautiful daughter, Mrs. Meirowitz, and she gave me the honor of taking her picture at the beach," he said as he bent over slightly to bow.

"I told her that I would make one for her and deliver it, so here it is, and also a little gift for her." He pulled off the cloth. The box turned out to be a cage and a beautiful parrot was bobbing on his perch.

"This is a young bird that will take on the speech of the family and can be taught to say anything. Do you think Nettie will like it, Mrs. Meirowitz?"

Golda loved every living creature and she was amazed at this colorful bird. "I can't allow her to accept this gift," she said as she looked at the parrot and tried to conceal her own longing for the bird.

"Please madam, let me leave this for her. I'm so grateful to her for the picture. My boss was very pleased with me. I don't know if he will use it, but he appreciated my effort. Let her have it, Mrs. Meirowitz, she will enjoy him."

She will enjoy him, he says. I'll enjoy him, she thought as her heart was beating with excitement.

She forced herself to act calmly and she quietly answered him, "I thank you and I will tell her what you said. And now, if you will excuse me, I have had a very busy day."

"Of course," he said. "It was a pleasure to talk to you. Please give my regards to Nettie and thank her again."

As soon as he left, Golda took the cage into the house and studied the bird. He was green with yellow, blue and a bit of black. What a beauty, she thought. Out loud, she said to the bird, "Welcome to our home. I hope you'll start talking like he said."

To her delight, the bird called out, "Hello, hello."

As the family came home, each one admired Polly and talked to him. It didn't take too many days for Polly to learn to say, "Polly wants a cracker," and "Vey is meir" (*woe is me*).

The family was delighted, especially Golda. She took good care of the bird, kept his cage clean, gave him fresh water, his seeds and sometimes gave him a slice of apple. She enjoyed having him. Joey loved to sleep and had a hard time getting up. Golda always had to call him many times. "Joey, get up. Everybody goes to work."

One morning, Polly started to shout, "Joey, Joey, get up, get up. Everybody goes to work."

"Shut up," shouted Joey and he threw a slipper at the cage, and Polly screamed, "Gevalt, vey is meir."

Golda kept the cover on Polly until she woke Joe up by going into his room and waking him up herself, and the mornings were quiet after that.

****

Amy and Millie were four and half years apart and even though the family was close, these two were a unit unto themselves. They played together, Amy always taking care of her little sister, teaching her, dressing her. They were called those two, the Bobsey twins, and the pixilated pair by their brothers and sisters. They had a very happy childhood. They adored and were in awe of their big sister, Claire. They would do anything she asked.

One Sunday morning, Claire, who was in charge of cleaning the dining and front rooms, presented each girl with a balloon, a red one for Amy and a green one for Millie. She had been to a party the night before and thought they would enjoy having them. Of course they were thrilled that Claire thought of them.

"Now I'll teach you how to do an arabesque, kids," she said.

"You hold the balloon in one hand and raise that hand as high as you can, bend down, lift your right leg up and, with your other hand, you dust the legs of the furniture with this cloth."

They were glad to do anything for her, went on errands, doing whatever she asked. She loved them and was proud of them.

One Saturday when she returned home from work, Claire found out that there was going to be a block party and there would be a children's beauty contest. She made a Cupid's costume for Millie. She draped a piece of chiffon, edged with pearls around her torso. She made her a headdress of the same material, and made a bow and arrow out of a hanger, covered it with ribbon and sent her to the contest. Millie won first prize, which was a kewpie doll.

Millie was so happy because she never had a store bought doll. Golda had always made the girls rag dolls. Amy and Millie, loved them, gave them names and played house with them. They didn't have store bought toys, but not too many children had a brother like Harry who bought them double runner ice skates and took them to Prospect Park to skate.

****

Harry came into the kitchen for his breakfast and smiled as he stirred his coffee. "Mom, Poppa, I have some news for you."

"Tell us. Tell us" exclaimed Golda, who always got excited at good news.

Harry slowly put his spoon down and took a sip of his coffee as if to prolong the announcement and then said, "I found a car, a very good buy. It is a Cadillac, as good as new. Adolph, Henry, and I will learn to drive, and get our licenses. It will be nice to take you, Mom, and the kids for a drive. What do you think, Papa?"

Golda didn't wait for her husband to respond. "A car? A machine? An automobile? I can't believe what I'm hearing. I would be afraid to sit in one and to put my children in one of those things. Oy vey Harry, where did you get such an idea?"

"Mom, its safe, and you will love it." Harry went to his mother and kissed her.

"Mom, I want you to have pleasure, nothing is too good for my Mom. So, Pop, should we buy it? It's worth the money and I can afford it."

Pincas was enjoying the display of affection and caring by Harry to his mother. He was a good son, respectful, helpful, and capable. Always ready to take care of any problem in the family. He was touched to think that Harry would ask for his approval to buy the car.

"Harry," he said, "I think it would be fine if you're sure it's safe."

Harry was delighted. "Good, I'll take care of everything. I know how to drive. I'll make an appointment for a test and I'll get my license. In no time our car will be here," he said confidently.

Pincas smiled at his enthusiasm. All his boys were fine young men. He was a very strict father, demanding respect and obedience from them as they grew up. They were taught Hebrew at an early age by a good teacher who came to the house. They bound their "tefillen" on their arms every morning after their Bar Mitzvah. They were helpful in the house and showed love and caring for their sisters.

"Golda, we did a good job on our boys," Pincas remarked when Harry left. "All men in America aren't so considerate of their parents. I hear a lot when I'm in the Place. We are lucky, and I thank G-D."

"And the girls? You don't find such daughters around either, G-d bless them," answered Golda proudly.

One summer evening around suppertime, Harry drove into the driveway. Everyone came out. They were amazed to see such a beautiful car. Amy and Millie jumped up and down and the rest of the family stood in awe. It was a tourist car. It was open and had no windows. It could seat five or six if three sat in the front. It had a spare tire on the back of the car. There were window covers that could snap on if there was rain or heavy wind.

Harry opened the door of this shiny car and said very grandly, "Mom and Poppa please step in. You are the first to have a ride."

"Oh, let the two little girls come too," said Golda, "Come Amy, come Millie. As they rode away the rest of the family applauded and shouted hurrah.

The car was highly polished after every trip, which was every Sunday afternoon if it didn't rain. The car was never used in the rain. It was a delightful luxury enjoyed by the whole family. Golda would take a bag full of challah rolls and hand them out as they rode along. Pincas sat proudly in the front seat. Golda and a few of the children sat in the back. They never crowded in the car. Pincas wouldn't allow a strain on the car. Harry or Henry never took the car out of the garage without their father's knowledge and consent. It was a prized possession not to be abused or taken for granted.

"Poppa, I'm going to the movies with Claire and Henry tonight. Is that okay with you? We'll go by car." Harry had come into his parents' bedroom to ask, and when he saw the pain on his father's face, he felt sad. He would do or give anything if he could make Poppa feel better. He loved this man, his father, and had deep respect for him. The car was considered Poppa's even though Harry paid for it. It was in the name of Pincas Meirowitz.

Pincas was unwinding his foot bandage and getting ready for bed. He smiled at his son. Such a good boy, he thought, asking me permission to use the car. Aloud he said, "Just be careful, go safely and come home safely," and he added, "have a good time."

"Don't worry," Harry said as the three of them started out. The children all got along very well and enjoyed being together.

"That was a great movie," stated Claire as they were leaving the theater. Did you enjoy it?"

Henry and Harry both agreed it was a good film and they started for the car.

"I'm sure I parked it right here didn't I?" asked Harry.

They quietly walked around the parking lot fearing the worst. Could it have been stolen? The lot was almost empty by now and no sign of the car.

"I better look for a cop and report this," said Harry. He found an officer and, after giving a description and all the information about the car, he accepted the offer from the policeman to drive them home.

"What will we tell Papa?" asked Claire.

The boys looked at each other and finally Henry said, "Claire, you tell him, you'll know how."

Claire thought for a minute and said, "I'll tell the truth, exactly what happened. What else can I tell him?" Harry and Henry nodded and soon they were home.

"Children is that you? Did you enjoy the movie? Come up and tell Momma and me about it," called Pincas.

They came up but only Claire entered the room. "Poppa I have to tell you something", she said softly. One look at the sad and troubled face of his daughter and Pincas knew the news wasn't good.

"What happened? Was there an accident? Were the boys hurt? Oh, dear lord, tell me what happened?" he groaned.

"No Poppa, nothing like that. The boys are fine and so am I. You see, here they are."

Harry and Henry came into the room.

"Oh thank G-d, that's the most important thing. You are all safe. Nothing is more important than that!" exclaimed Pincas gratefully.

"The car was stolen," stated Claire.

"What? Stolen? How? Oh my goodness what happened?"

"Papa, please don't be so upset. You said that all that matters is that we are unharmed. I know it's hard to bear, but please don't carry on so," pleaded Claire.

Pincas was quiet for a minute then he said, "G-d bless you my child, of course you are right, G-d forgive me for being so foolish. Boys don't feel so bad. Perhaps the car will be found. No matter, let's go to bed."

Golda was quiet all this time, concerned for her husband and children. She hugged her two sons and her daughter and said, "I 'm so proud of all of you, now do as Poppa says. Go to sleep."

When the children left, Golda kissed her husband. "Pina," she said, "I know how shocked and sad you are. I love the way you spoke to Claire. That was a lesson for them and for us as well."

The next day the car was found in a lot, stripped of every thing. Just the shell remained. They accepted the insurance money, but that was the end of the Cadillac and a car for them until some years later.

****

The house was a dream come true for Golda. Her tomatoes were most delicious. She kept a saltshaker on the windowsill near the hose. The children and their friends would take a tomato, wash it, shake some salt on it, and really enjoy eating it. This gave Golda so much pleasure. "It's worth all my work to see the children eat fresh and healthy food," she would say.

Golda made it a habit to look in the window of the pet shop whenever she went shopping. She loved to see the little dogs, the different small animals, and sometimes she would go in and touch them. The owner knew her and made her feel welcome.

"Come in Mrs. Meirowitz, I want to show you something." He took her over to a large carton that contained many little newly hatched chicks huddled together.

"Oh, how darling, look at them," she said, "like little balls of yellow wool. John, do people buy them? And how much do they cost?'

"Of course people buy them," he laughed. "I can give you a very good price if you are interested."

Golda was thinking. We could keep them in the kitchen on the desk. And when they got bigger, we would build a nice chicken coop and they would lay eggs. It would be fun for the children.

"I'll ask my husband, and if he says yes, I'll be back," she said.

Golda was so excited she forgot to ask how much it would cost, and as her children came home, she told them about the chicks. They all shared her enthusiasm. Now she would ask Pina when he came home from work. She just couldn't wait for him to make himself comfortable.

"Pina, they have the cutest little chicks in the pet store. The children would love to have them. When they get a little bigger, we could build a chicken coop, and they will lay eggs. Oh, Pina, I would love to have them. I didn't ask how much they cost, but I'm sure it will be inexpensive and well worth it." She was almost breathless with excitement.

Pina sat down wearily, stretching his foot out and even though he was in pain, he had to laugh at his wife. She was so dear. "Goldala, Goldala, if you want to have chickens, have them, it's fine with me. You work so hard, why look for more responsibility?"

"Oh, I don't mind at all. I'll go to the store tomorrow and give John my order."

When the chicks were delivered, one hundred of them, Golda had already prepared a large corrugated box with a light over it for warmth. The chicks tumbled on top of each other as they were lowered into the box, making little clucking sounds.

They grew and were soon old enough for the waiting chicken coop. The boys made a screened area from the entrance of the coop to a nice size of the backyard, allowing the chickens to walk around. Golda dug the ground up so they could find some worms and just peck and scratch around. They did lay eggs and it was fun to find them. Joey really enjoyed going to the coop and feeding the chickens. He knew all of them and gave some of them names.

Amy and Millie had goldfish, Nettie had Polly (really Golda had Polly), and now there were chickens. They all became part of the household.

When she was finished with the housework, Golda would sit on the porch and admire her beautiful rosebush. When the petals were about to fall off, Golda would make rose jelly.

One day Amy and Millie were coming out of the house, and there were two boys about to take some roses. Amy said in a loud voice, "I'm going to call my big brother and you'll be very sorry that you're taking my mother's roses. Harry, Harry."

By the time she called a second time, the boys had fled. Harry wasn't even home, but Amy knew that just mentioning his name was enough to scare those boys away.

****

Pincas came into the kitchen. When Golda saw his face, she knew there was trouble.

"What is it, Pina? What happened?" She was drying a dish, and, as she put it down, she started to twist the towel.

"Golda, we must go to see Mama. She's very sick. I called up to talk to them and a woman answered. She told me that they were about to call us and tell us to come. Golda, I'm worried," he said.

Golda had already taken off her apron and started to call the children. "We have to go to Bubba and Zaida. Get dressed and please, children, hurry."

"Oh, Pina," she said, tears streaming down her cheeks, "I love her. She is my mother, too. I hardly remember my own mother. Maybe it's not as serious as the neighbors said, please G-d."

On the train Golda sat with Amy and Millie. Nettie, Henry and Joey were with Pincas. The others would follow when they came home.

"Mama," asked Amy, "why were you crying? You don't cry when one of us gets sick."

Golda put one arm around Amy and the other around Millie, hugged them and answered, "My darlings, when a child gets sick with a temperature, or a stomach ache, it usually isn't serious, but when a Bubba gets sick and the doctor calls for the family, it is." Her eyes were over-brimming with tears as she drew her two little girls to her.

Nothing more was said and soon they arrived at the apartment. Ida, Helen and Moe were already there, and they all embraced quietly. There were men praying in a corner of the room. Solomon was with them. Rachael was breathing with difficulty and trying to say something, but couldn't.

Golda went over to the bed, took Rachael's hand, kissed it, and said softly, "Mama, all your children are here, Ida, Helen, Moe, Pina, the grandchildren, we are here. We love you." Tears

65

were flowing as she held and patted Rachael's hand.

Suddenly, the breathing slowed down and it became very quiet in the room. A few minutes later, Rachael closed her eyes and died.

Helen, Ida and Golda held on to each other and cried.

Ida said, "Golda, Mama loved you and you were so good to her and Papa. Poor Papa," she went on, "what's he going to do?"

"He's welcome to live with us," Golda said. "We have room and the shul is not too far. After this is over, the funeral and the shiva week of mourning, we'll see what he wants to do."

The children were frightened at the death of their grandmother. They had never seen anyone die before and it was a trauma for them. Pincas was aware of them and called them into the kitchen.

"Children," he said, "maybe your mother and I were wrong to allow you to be here at a time like this, but this is part of living. We must learn to accept G-d's will. Bubba has had a good life, a long life. She did what made her happy, taking care of people who were poor and needed help. Remember the good times we had on Saturday nights after the Havdalah service at her lavah malkas, the party that prolongs the beautiful feeling of Shabbat. Remember how the old men from the shul enjoyed the food she served them and the singing and dancing you children did? That's what we have to do, remember the good things, the happy times. Also, we want to be considerate of Zaida. He will need a lot of comforting and love."

The funeral was well attended. There were quite a few young women who had been the recipients of Rachael's generosity when their babies were born. They told Helen, Ida, Golda, and Pincas all the things Rachael had done for them.

"She never made us feel that we were charity cases," said one of the women.

"May she rest in peace," said another. "We'll miss her."

The week of mourning was held in Solomon and Rachael's home. The family stayed together. When the week was over and the family had taken a walk around the block, they sat down and tried to make plans for Solomon.

But Solomon had his own plans. He had thought about it during the period of shiva and now spoke to his children.

"Children, my dear son and daughters, I know you are concerned for me and I love you for it. I have made up my mind. I will stay here in my home. Please don't worry. I'll be fine. I have friends and I will manage."

Golda became alarmed. "Papa," she said, "How will you manage? You can't even boil water for your tea? Oh, this will never do. Please let us take care of you."

"Mine tierer kind (*my precious child*)," he said, looking lovingly at his daughter-in-law, "I have loved you from the first time I saw you in your Tanta's home, remember?"

Solomon smiled as he thought of the shy, little girl that stood before him in Romania.

"You were so frightened. I knew you would be happy with my son and would be a good wife. I was right. You have been good to him, to your wonderful children and to Mama and me. I thank you from the bottom of my heart, but I'll remain in my own home," he said gently.

Pina was standing in the doorway of the kitchen, leaning on his cane. His leg was hurting from the walk and he couldn't wait to take off the brace and lie down on a bed. "Papa," he said, "if that's what you want, try it, but you must promise that if you find it hard, you'll tell us and we will work something out."

"Absolutely, my son, thank you. Go, get off your feet, lie down," he said with deep concern.

"Thank you, Papa. That's just what I'll do. Golda, do you think the little ones can go home with the others and we will stay with Papa, tonight?"

"That's a very good idea Pina," Golda said approvingly. I'll give Joey some money, and when they get home he'll buy a malted, and some candy treats and everyone will be happy."

"Come Amy, Millie, Joey, and Nettie. Poppa and I are going to stay with Zaida tonight and you will go home. Nettie and Joey will take charge. Be good and go safely," said Golda as she kissed each child.

The next day Golda made some breakfast for them and said to her father-in-law, "Poppa before we leave I'll make some soup for you, but Poppa, please come to us for a while. If you must live here, at least visit us often. O.K.? I worry about you."

"I will, I will my darling," answered Solomon stroking Golda's serious face. "Don't worry. I'll be fine and I will come."

Solomon did come and everyone was so happy. The children loved this gentle man and Amy and Millie always stroked his soft flowing beard. "Zadie tell us a story about the old country," they would beg. "Tell us about how Mamma was when you met her."

"Again?" Golda was listening and now she laughed. "How many times do you have to hear that? To tell the truth, I like to hear it too," she added, looking with affection at the man who helped change her life.

****

One morning Solomon entered the kitchen as Golda was kneading dough for her challah. "Good morning Poppa, did you sleep well? Are you ready for breakfast? I'll just finish with this dough and serve you." She gave the dough one last pat, put some oil on her hands and then on the dough, covered it with a towel and set it on one of the counters to rise.

Golda took great pride in her kitchen. It was her favorite room, the one where she spent most of her time. It was large and white. It had a small table which was used for cooking and baking and a large one for the family. Golda kept her kitchen spotless. Her aluminum pots were shiny. The glasses, dishes and flatware glistening, Golda always had fruit in a basket on the large table so the family would be tempted and eat it. In one corner there was a backless chair. The hand grinder could be attached to the seat to grind the fish for gefilte fish.

"Goldala," Solomon said, "I wonder if you have time to make something for me."

"Poppa, you know I would do anything for you. What is it that you want?" asked Golda eagerly.

"I have a craving for a very delicate chicken soup. Would you make me some from one of the chickens in the backyard?"

Golda almost dropped the bowl of oatmeal she was bringing to the table. She started to twist her apron. Oh, she thought, how could she take one of her pets to be slaughtered, and then cook it? And yet how could she refuse Poppa? This dear man, if it weren't for him, she would still be at Toba's. She wouldn't have her dear husband and her wonderful children. All that she had, she owed to him.

"Yes, Poppa, I'll be glad to do it. You eat your oatmeal. I'll serve you coffee and then I'll go." As soon as she served Solomon and washed the dishes, she slowly took off her apron, hung it on the hook in back of the door, picked up her shopping bag and said, "Poppa, I'll be home as fast as I can."

She went out to the chicken coop and sadly looked at the chickens. Which one should I take? Oh, why did I buy them? "I can't do it," she said aloud.

Then she thought, how can I refuse Poppa? I must respect him and do what he asks. She grabbed the nearest chicken, and with trembling hands tied his feet and put him in her bag.

As she walked to the market she thought of Joe. Oh, what will he say when he finds out? What I've done to poor Joey! He loves these chickens. He'll be heartbroken.

She arrived at the market and went to the section where the Sherchet, the rabbi who slaughters fowl, was located. She handed him the chicken and he performed the rituals and then gave the bird to a woman whose job it was to remove the feathers from the chicken.

When the woman handed the bag to Golda, it was warm and Golda was very upset. She paid the fee and hurried out of the store. As she quickly walked home, she felt the bag and it's warmth bobbing against her leg. She couldn't stop the tears from flowing down her cheeks. Oh dear Lord, she thought, what have I done?

When she came home, Golda worked quickly and steadily so as not to think about the happenings of the day. The soup was cooking, and the smell was different from the usual chicken soup smell. Usually, she made soup out of a pullet. This was a very young, spring chicken, and it was different.

At three thirty, Joe came home from school. "What is that smell Mamma?" he asked. "What are you cooking? It smells awful."

"Oh, it's soup for Zaida," she said trying to sound matter of fact.

"What kind of soup Mama?" he persisted.

Golda looked at her son's face and she saw fear in it as if he knew the answer.

"Joey, Zaida asked me to make him some chicken soup from one of our chickens. I couldn't refuse him. Please Joey, don't be angry with him or me. Zaida is weak and old, and he thinks this soup will give him strength."

Joe didn't answer. Instead he went out to the coop and counted the chicks. He knew which one was missing. He stayed out in the backyard for a long while, and then went to his room to do his homework.

That evening Golda called the family for dinner as soon as Pincas came home. Joe sat very quietly with his head down and his hands in his lap. When Mama served the soup, tears trickled down his cheeks as he refused to eat anything. When dinner was over, Golda was very upset. She felt even worse when she saw his sad, pinched face.

"Come in the kitchen, Joey, I want to talk to you."

Joey said, "I really don't want to talk about it," but he reluctantly followed her into the kitchen.

"Please listen to me, Joey. It hurts me, too. I can't go on like this. I am going to get rid of the chickens and the coop. I will sell them to the egg man, he will be glad to have them. And Joey, please know that I am very sorry."

She gave him a hug, and he left the room quietly.

1921

It was the month of September and the holiday of Sukkot, the Feast of Tabernacles was approaching. It was time for the boys and Pina to build their sukkah. They made three sides; the fourth wall was the house. The opening faced the back door to make it easy to bring food in from the kitchen. The decorations were left to Golda and the children. Amy and Nettie made pictures and helped hang fruits and gourds from the trellised ceiling. Amy encouraged Millie to make some pictures too and she was delighted.

The boys enjoyed working with their father. Pina was a stern man and while he was kind, fair, and loved his sons, he was strict with them. They loved and respected him and always enjoyed working on any project with him. Pincas made the building of the sukkah a real fun day. They ate outside picnic-style. Golda brought out sandwiches and drinks and later fruit and cookies.

Al was engaged to Claire and loved this family. He was an orphan, who lived with his uncle and aunt. His uncle was a plumber and, after graduation from Cooper Union, Al became a plumber's helper. He was very smart and good with his hands. He was a great help building the sukkah. He told Pincas, "Some day I'm going to make a collapsible sukkah. It will be easier."

They completed the sukkah and created a roof of sweet-smelling leaves and flowers. The family ate all their meals in the sukkah. The sky above could be seen through the leaves and flowers both day and night. There was seldom a day that the family didn't have guests with whom to share the sukkah. Men from the shul, friends of the children, neighbors—all were welcome. Some came in the morning to bench etrog (*to say a prayer with the etrog, which looks like an oversized lemon, and lulav, a palm branch with leaves of the myrtle and willow.*) The prayer they said praised G-d for the loving kindness he bestowed upon the Israelites by protecting them from harm when they lived in frail booths on their journey from Egypt through the wilderness.

****

The house was a joy for Golda, but it was also a great deal of work. She did the cooking, baking, shopping, and cleaning and never complained. The children helped. The boys washed the windows, did the heavy work, and the girls helped in the kitchen.

Golda treasured all living creatures. She would leave a saucer of milk outside the back door in case a dog or cat would be hungry. She scattered breadcrumbs for the birds. Just as she adored the parrot that had been given to Nettie, she encouraged the other children to have pets.

Joey loved pigeons and made a study of homing pigeons. Golda helped him buy what he wanted. The boys helped him make a pigeon coop and he would spend hours tying messages on the birds' legs, sending them off and waiting for their return. He was very happy with his pets.

"Harry," called Henry. "Joey is crying. Some wise guy is fooling around with his pigeons. I think he stole one or is holding it just to tease the kid."

"Oh, yeah?" Harry sounded defiant. He went quickly out to the backyard where Joey was sadly stroking one of his pigeons.

"Joey, tell me who the guy is. Where does he live? I'll take care of him. Don't worry; he'll never touch one of your pigeons again when I get through with him."

Joey was a very deep feeling boy. He was quiet and disliked fighting or confrontations. "Harry, please don't hurt him. Just scare him so he'll let my pigeons alone," he pleaded.

"Just leave it to me. No one is gonna hurt my family when I'm around," he said as he ruffed up Joey's hair.

Joey looked at his brother with admiration and love. What a guy, he thought. I'm lucky to have such a big brother.

Harry left, and in a little while he returned with a tall boy who had very red cheeks and appeared to be frightened.

"Tell my brother that you'll never touch his pigeons again," demanded Harry.

"Oh, I won't, I promise. I was only kidding," he quickly answered.

"Okay, beat it," said Harry roughly. The boy ran as fast as he could.

"He won't bother you anymore," assured Harry as he went into the house.

And so it was, neither that boy nor anyone else ever tried to hurt Joey or his pigeons. He enjoyed his birds for about a year or two, and then he decided to sell them coop and all to some boys.

****

"Golda, for Adolph's 21st birthday, I'm going to put him in business. I think that he is ready. He's learned a great deal from Moe and I think it's the right time."

Adolph was just thrilled. "Papa," he said, "I'm so grateful. Are you sure you can do that? Maybe you should take care of your foot instead of putting me in business. Remember that man who came to the house and talked of an operation and prosthesis for the whole foot? Papa, it's more important to spend money on that than on my business."

Pincas put his arm around his son. "Adolph, I'm so proud of you. You are everything that a man could want for a son, good, intelligent, sensitive, a very special person, a real mensch. A mensch is decent and good, a person of high regard, and that is what you are. I'm not ready for any operations, but I am ready to put my son into business.

Adolph smiled, gave his father a hug and said, "The window will read: **Pincas Meirowitz and Sons**."

"No, my son, I will not have my name in your business because you will open for business on the Shabbat. Instead it will say: **Adolph Meirowitz and Brothers**."

The store was opened and was doing very well. They sold silks and velvets. The boys and Pincas worked hard and were happy together. Pincas sat in the front, greeted the customers, and took care of the people who came in for donations for the poor, for schools, churches, synagogues, or for a handout. He never turned any of them down. He didn't give a great deal, but he said, "If one puts out a hand and the cause is good, you give regardless of faith or color." He was also quite active making packages of samples that the delivery boys hand-delivered.

Henry was an asset to the business. He had a way about him that endeared the customers. He was an excellent salesman and worked hard.

Adolph, soft spoken, always a gentleman, was a good businessman, and with Harry, who was very fair and honest but wouldn't let anyone be late for a payment, they had a successful and thriving business.

Golda would always supply lunch for all of them. "What's for lunch today, Mom?" Henry would ask.

"Surprise," Golda would answer. And every day it was a Kaiser roll with cream cheese and black olives. It was tasty and they enjoyed it, but it became a joke. Henry would ask the same question every day and the answer was always the same.

It was crowded on the Culver Line train in the morning. People were pushing to get a seat and to find a place to stand. There was barely space to open a newspaper. Harry always managed to find a seat for Pincas. He would move quickly when the doors opened, grab a seat, and wait for his father to come in.

"Here I am, Pop," Harry would say. Pincas would gratefully sit down holding the box of lunch.

One morning, as Pincas was sitting with the lunch, a man came over and demanded the box saying, "That's my box."

Pincas told him that it was a box of sandwiches. The man insisted that it was his box and was about to take it from Pincas. Harry was standing not too far away from his father and saw this man bothering Pincas. He pushed his way over and asked the man, "What is the trouble?"

"He's got my box and won't give it back to me," he said as he tried to take it again.

The train was just stopping at DeKalb Avenue, a longer stop than most stations since the train empties out there. Harry told this man that it was his father's box, and when the man continued to insist, Harry pushed him to the open door, gave him a powerful punch in the mouth, and said, "Leave my father alone."

The man did not come back on the train and the rest of the trip to New York City was without incident.

"Harry," Pincas said, "you really hit that man so hard, he lost a tooth. I saw him spit it out. You always use your fists instead of talking. I pray you shouldn't get into trouble because of it."

"Don't worry about it, Papa. I never hit anyone unless it's to protect my family, especially my Mom and Pop."

****

"Golda, I must talk to you. Please come into the front room." Pina and the boys had just come home from work and they were washing up for dinner.

"What is it, Pina? What happened? Oy vey, you call me into the front room, something terrible or something wonderful has or will be happening, but you're not smiling. Please tell me what is it?'"

"I didn't tell Adolph yet, I wanted to speak to you first."

"A Mr. Finkelstein came into the store today and after he introduced himself, he told me that he is a matchmaker. He was here to see me on behalf of Mr. and Mrs. Abromowitz. They have a daughter who is beautiful, bright, and with many virtues. He looked around the store and was very impressed. He said that our Adolph was recommended to them as a desirable suitor for their daughter. He also told me that they were Romanian and very nice people. So, Golda, what do you think? Should I talk to him? Meet them first? What should I do?"

Golda was smiling by now. As long as it wasn't a tragedy, no one hurt or in danger, she was relieved. "Pina," she said, "I think that you should tell him, and if he is willing, we should meet the parents first. If they seem to be balabatish (*fine, dependable people*), we will arrange a meeting."

"Good, that's the right way to do it. Nu, Golda, what do you say? Our son is soon to be a chuson (*bridegroom*)."

"It's just a meeting. He's not getting married yet. He's such a wonderful boy. He'll make a good husband and father. Pina, can you imagine him a father?" she asked. She became very serious and said, "I only hope she, or whoever he does marry, will be a fine person and love him. He's such a good, kind boy; I pray he should have a happy life."

Pina put his arm around Golda and kissed the top her head. "He will, with G-d's help. Tomorrow I'll talk to Adolph and then call Mr. Finkelstein."

It was early in the morning and Adolph was already dressed. He was putting on his watch when Pincas entered the room. "Good morning, my son. All ready for work?" Pincas was so proud of him. Golda is right, he thought to himself. This is a wonderful boy, handsome, clean-cut, smart, good as gold.

Out loud he said, "Adolph, a Mr. Finkelstein came to me and wanted to know if you would be interested in meeting a very nice girl. If yes, then Mama and I would first meet the family. So, son, what do you think?"

Adolph was taken aback for a moment, and then he smiled shyly. "I guess so, Papa, that is; I don't know what to say."

Pina laughed at his son. "Don't be embarrassed, son. It's natural for you to want to meet girls. If you aren't impressed with the young lady, there is no obligation."

"Papa," Adolph burst out, "she probably won't be impressed with me."

Pincas looked at his son and smiled. "Dear boy, don't you realize how desirable you are? You are handsome, well educated, a good businessman with a growing business. Who could want more than that?"

"Well, thank you, Papa, so when will I meet her?'

Pina said, "As soon as Mama and I meet with her parents. If it looks good, you'll call her and plan to meet. Is that all right with you?"

"Okay, Papa. Now I must get going. There is so much to do in the Place. I'll see you and the boys later. Don't let them be late. We are going to be busy today."

"Don't worry, we'll be there."

Pincas spoke to Golda before going to work. "Well," Pina said, "he was receptive, so if Mr. Finkelstein comes into the store, I'll make the appointment."

Golda and Pincas dressed carefully so as to make a good impression on Mr. and Mrs. Abromowitz. They lived on Orchard Street on the Eastside. They had a pushcart, and drew a meager living from it. They had three daughters and two sons. The oldest son was a doctor, but was not practicing. They didn't say why and Golda and Pina didn't question them.

Mrs. Abromowitz did all the talking, telling Golda and Pincas all about their lovely daughter, how well bred, soft-spoken and obedient she was. She was a fine girl who helped in the house and had a very nice job. Her boss was just crazy about her.

"He's just meshuga for her," she said.

Her husband, his name was Sissa, started to say something, but his wife silenced him with a stern, "Sha, she will be home soon and you will meet her. Tell me, does the whole family work in the store?" she asked sweetly.

"No," Pina answered, "just the boys and I. Our oldest daughter is engaged and is a bookkeeper for a large concern, and the rest are in school." Just then, the door opened and a very pretty girl entered the room.

"Hi," she said. She was smiling, and seemed pleasant. Golda observed her medium height, her small blue eyes, her blond hair and good figure. She was sure that Adolph would be pleased.

"This is our daughter, Jean," Eva Abromowitz proudly said. "And Jeanala, this is Mr. and Mrs. Meirowitz. They have a very handsome son that they would like you to meet."

Jean looked at them shyly and said, "How do you do?"

Golda was sure that she knew about Adolph, no doubt passed the store and saw him a few times, but she said nothing. Instead, she answered, "Very well, thank you, and how do you do?"

Pincas smiled approvingly and said, "With your permission, my son will call you to arrange a meeting. It was nice to meet you my dear. Come, Golda, we should leave. Thank you, Mr. and Mrs. Abromowitz."

"Oh, are you leaving so soon? I didn't even offer you a cup of tea," Eva said. "You must think I'm a poor hostess."

"Not at all. Golda and I really have to get home. The children are alone, but thank you and we hope to meet again," Pina's answered.

"So, Mama, Papa, how was it? Did you see the girl? Is she pretty? Fat? Tall? Did she say anything about meeting me? Tell me, tell me." Adolph was talking so fast that he was almost breathless.

"Calm down, son," Pina said laughingly. "Mama and I had a pleasant time and yes, we did meet Jean. Golda, tell him what you think."

Golda looked at her son and smiled. He seemed so young, so eager, and yet she sensed his nervousness. She thought, this boy is so vulnerable. I'm worried.

Aloud she said, "She's very pretty, well-mannered, seemed anxious to meet you. We didn't spend too much time with her, just greetings. We'll give you her phone number, you'll call her, make an appointment to meet, and you'll see for yourself."

It took him a few days to muster up the courage to call her, but he did. She made it so easy and pleasant that he was just delighted. They had a wonderful time, and made plans to see each other again.

"Pina," Golda said as she brought the coffee to the table, "have you noticed a change in Adolph? I think he's in love with Jean.

Pincas smiled and said, as he stirred the sugar in his coffee, "I think so, too. Let's not say too much to him about the girl. Let's wait for him to tell us. I don't want to push him. Aye, Golda, America is different from Romania. There a father finds a match for his son and that's the way it is. Here, in America, it's he loves her; she loves him, and fartig (*that's that*). For you and me the old way worked out just fine, right, my Goldala?"

"Right," she answered as she reminisced. She closed her eyes and saw herself standing before Papa, so fearful that she wouldn't please him, and that she wouldn't get away from Toba. "Oh yes, Pina, for us it was perfect. Couldn't be better."

"She came into the store today and you should have seen your son. He was so proud as he showed her his stock and everything. Yes, he's in love and he'll tell us soon," Pincas said.

"Pina," Golda asked, "do you think there will be a noden (*a dowry*)?"

I really don't know," Pina said. "Usually the poorest parents provide some noden for their daughter. Who knows? We'll see."

"When our girls get married they will have a beautiful oushtah (*trousseau*), right, Pina?" Golda asked.

Pincas smiled at his wife. How sweet she was. She never wanted or needed anything for herself, just for him, the children and anyone else who needed help.

Aloud he said, "Of course we will, as much as we possibly can. Before we know it, we'll be planning their weddings."

"They are so beautiful. They'll be snatched up. Remember when Claire told me that she didn't want a matchmaker like Mr. Finkelstein. Oy, she is something," Pina said proudly. "She said, 'in America people meet each other, and if they fall in love, they marry.'"

Golda became apprehensive. "Maybe we shouldn't have acted so quickly with Adolph. You know, Pina, he never went out with any girls before Jean, so how can he be sure?"

"Golda, don't worry. He's not getting married so soon. He didn't say anything to us yet. We'll wait until he does."

It was Sunday morning. The whole family was still asleep, except Pincas and Golda. They were enjoying their morning coffee on the porch. It was restful for them. They loved to listen to the birds, the sounds of stirring outside, the gentle rustling of the trees in the quiet, free from the noise of automobiles, of horse drawn milk wagons, no disturbance. They hardly spoke to each other, just sat quietly sipping coffee.

"Good morning, Mama, Papa. Oh, it's so beautiful here in the morning. I hope I'm not intruding."

Golda smiled at her son. "No, dear, it's all right. Come sit down with us. Is everything okay with you? Did you have a good time last night?"

"Yes, I did. I always have a great time when I'm with Jeannie." Golda and Pincas exchanged quick looks and waited.

"Mama, Papa, we want to get married. Is that okay with you? Her parents are very pleased. I think they like me." Adolph looked hopefully at his parents.

"They told me I had a very pretty mother and a fine father, as if I didn't know that," he said hugging his mother.

Pincas tried to put his son at ease. "Sure," he said mockingly, "a very pretty mother, but not a handsome father, just fine."

"Oh, Papa." Adolph was laughing now and bit more relaxed. "They really like you. So what do you think?"

Golda said, "Like Papa said the other day, this is America and it's different. Parents don't pick the mates for their children. I only want you to be happy and to have a good life. If you are sure that she is the one for you, and she feels the same way, then we are satisfied, right, Pina?"

"Right. Now tell us, when is this great day going to be?"

"Pretty soon. Mrs. Abromowitz says, 'What's the sense of waiting?' So we'll look for an apartment and then make arrangements. Thank you for making it so easy for me, Mom and Pop. I love you."

"Oy, my Alteral," Golda said, "I wish I could make your life beautiful and happy. What about the wedding? Have you talked about it?"

"First, I have to buy Jeannie an engagement ring. Will you go with me?"

"Of course. We'll go to the jewelers during our lunch hour," Pina said. "There is a ceremony for engagement. Two plates are broken to seal the commitment. Mama will invite them here and we'll do it, and we'll hear about the wedding plans."

"Oh wait, Papa, please don't talk about wedding plans. They are poor people. Jeannie and I will plan the wedding and I will pay for it, so please, I don't want to embarrass them, okay?"

Golda made a lovely dinner, knishes, bagelloch, braided phyllo dough filled with cheese, chopped eggplant, salad, rugelach, and coffee, a real Romanian meal.

"Just delicious," exclaimed Eva Abromowitz. Adolph was beaming and his brothers and sisters were happy for him.

"Now we will break the two plates to make the engagement binding, that is if the children are sure they want to be engaged," Pincas teased. Everyone laughed and Jean took Adolph's hand and kissed it. He responded by doing the same thing.

"Ready?" Pincas dropped the two plates. They broke with a loud thud. "Mazel tov, mazel tov." Everyone was so happy.

"We'll get married in June," Jean said softly. "Six months is enough time to arrange everything. Do you agree, Adolph?"

Adolph was looking at her with such love and pride that he could hardly speak. He nodded and finally said, "Fine with me, whatever you say."

It was time to leave. Kissing, blessings, and laughter filled the room. They all left, including Adolph, who wanted to see Jean home.

Golda and the girls started to clean up. "She's pretty," said Amy and then she picked up a basket that Golda used for socks that needed mending. She put it in Millie's hand and said, "Micky, you have to practice being the flower girl. I'll teach you how to walk and throw the petals."

Claire said, "Amy, you don't know if Jean will want her to be the flower girl, so wait until she is asked."

"Oh, I'm sure she'll ask her. Micky's the youngest in the family and a flower girl is always just a little kid," Amy said. Amy called her little sister Millie 'Micky.' She was the only one who did. She took care of her, dressed her, and they were very close and always together.

Plans for the wedding were made quickly. An apartment was rented and the excitement of preparation was prominent in the house. Dresses for Golda and the girls were made by a dressmaker. Amy and Millie would wear the same dresses. Claire designed her dress, and Nettie had the same dress as Jean's niece, Viola, because they were to be flower girls.

"Don't be disappointed, Micky. It's not that great to be a flower girl," Amy said as she hugged her sister.

PINCAS MEIROWITZ

Pincas was slowly unwinding his leg bandage in preparation for bed. It was a lengthy task, but tonight he didn't mind. His head was full of happy thoughts. His oldest son was getting married. He is such a boy, so good, so bright, a college graduate, and so handsome. He looks like his mother. Pincas smiled. I am a lucky man he thought. I have a wonderful wife, eight fine children, all healthy. Not one wears glasses. I make a living, thank the good lord. May I continue to be blessed.

His thoughts went to his soon to be daughter-in-law. A very pretty girl, well mannered, loves Adolph, nice family, Romanian, poor people but that doesn't matter. What's important is that she will be a good and caring wife.

He finished rolling up the bandage and placed it on the night table where he had all the things he needed for his foot and leg. The cream he used on his leg, the sponges he needed to line the brace and place his heel on them. The operation he had when he was very young left him with no toes. just a ball at the heel. These sponges were such a comfort to him.

His daughter Claire was in Woolworth one day and saw a display of sponges. She thought it might be soft for his foot. It proved to be good for him. His brace was so heavy and hard. G-d bless Claire, he would say to himself every time he used them.

Finally, he was ready to say his evening prayers before going to bed. He waited for his younger children to come in to recite the "Shma" with him. He loved this time and looked forward to it every night. Nettie, Amy and Millie would stand and say the prayer, then kiss their father and go to bed. He enjoyed seeing and listening to their sweet voices. He was so proud of his family.

Pincas was a religious man. He was kind, charitable, and never turned anyone down for a donation. He sat in the front of the store and always had small money handy for beggars or charity solicitors who came in. He would say, "If someone holds out his hand you must respond." That's the way he brought up his children.

He also lectured his children to be honest, trustworthy, and polite. They were. Sometimes Harry forgot his manners if anyone in his family was mistreated or threatened.

Pincas raised his boys with a firm hand. He loved them dearly and saw to it that they had good clothing. He wanted the best for them that he could afford, but expected good behavior and respect for their mother and himself. Pincas had the courage of his convictions. He said whatever he felt he had to whenever he thought it necessary. This didn't always sit too well with Golda.

"Pina, you can't tell people how to live, how to conduct their lives," she would tell him.

But it didn't matter. Pincas would say whatever he felt was right. For example, he was coming home from shul one Saturday morning and passed a neighbor who was Jewish. The man was gardening. Pincas stopped, watched for a minute or two and said politely, "Excuse me mister. Do you know it's Shabbos. You shouldn't be working in the garden. It's a sin."

The man was startled, smiled and then answered, "I'm not religious and I don't have time during the week." He continued to work.

"Well," said Pincas, "it's my duty to tell you, Good day." He proceeded to walk home.

When he came into the house Golda greeted him warmly. "Gut Shabbos, Pina. How was the service?"

Saturday afternoon was the time that Golda loved. It was peaceful and pleasant. No work. Pincas would tell her about the service at the shul, who was there and Golda was always interested.

"Gut Shabbos to you, Goldala. The service was fine. I was called to the torah," answered Pincas as he sat down heavily in the nearest chair. The shiny kitchen smelled of chicken soup and all the wonderful Sabbath food Golda would soon serve.

First, she placed a wine goblet and a platter of honey cake in front of him. "Nu, any news?" she asked. Golda loved to talk to her husband and he enjoyed telling her about the sermon or the torah reading .

"I'll tell you about the service. It was wonderful, but I must tell you about that new family that moved in a few months ago. Do you know them?" he asked. When Golda responded that she hadn't paid a call to the new neighbor yet, Pincas told her about his encounter with the man.

Golda was appalled. "How could you do such a thing? Why is everything your business? Oh Pina, I always beg you not to tell other people how to live. I'm so embarrassed. I was going over there to wish them good luck and welcome them. See? I have a cake ready to bring. Now I feel funny going over. Oh Pina," she said sadly.

Pincas held on to the table and pulled himself up. He recited the blessing over the wine, passed the goblet to Golda, took a piece of cake and slowly and carefully sat down again.

"Golda, I had to tell him," he said. "It's Shabbos and even if he isn't religious, it's a shonda (*shame*) for the neighbors. Golda, he'll take a bite of your cake and who knows? He might change his ways. Please don't be embarrassed. I did what I had to do. Where are the children?"

Golda looked at her husband and smiled. I'll never change him she thought. I don't want to spoil our Shabbos with my nagging.

"They are upstairs. They didn't hear you come in. I'll call them," she answered. She went to the foot of the stairs and called, "Amy, Nettie, Millie, Poppa is home, Come down."

"Gut Shabbos, Poppa." Amy, Millie, and Nettie came in and greeted their father with a kiss.

"Gut Shabbos, kinderloch," Pina responded warmly. "Let's eat."

That was a typical Saturday. After lunch, which consisted of delicious chicken noodle soup, chicken, kugel of potato or noodle, carrots, compote, tea and cake, the children would go to the movies. Pina would allow them to go as long as they purchased the tickets on Friday. Pina and Golda would retire to their bedroom until late afternoon and then enjoy the rest of the day at home to receive friends, drink tea, and talk.

Friends would walk over and Golda would set a sweet table. She put out homemade rugelach, sponge cake, mandelbroit, and served tea. She was so happy when people came to visit.

Pincas really loved the Sabbath. He regretted that his boys kept the store open. They had to; all the trade was open on Saturday. That was why he refused to have his name on the window or be involved in the business even though he put Adolph in it.

"Are you still awake, Pina?" Golda asked, as she came into their bedroom. Golda would never retire unless everything was washed and put away.

"I'm finished now and I'm ready to go to sleep. Gutta nocht mine tira vibe *(good night my dear wife)."*

****

The great wedding day finally arrived. Golda was so proud of her children. They all lookrd so handsome and were dressed very elegantly.

"Pina just look at our family. Kenahora, spare us from an evil eye. Each one is so beautiful."

"Yes, Goldala, they are. Please, G-d, may they have mazel, good luck. That's the most important thing. Come. Let's go. Adolph will worry if we are late."

The wedding was over. Everything went well. Everyone was happy. Jean and Adolph returned from a short honeymoon and settled in their apartment.

****

"Golda," Pincas said, "I don't like the way Adolph looks. He's pale and seems so nervous and strained. I hope everything is all right with them."

"Maybe he has to get used to being married. He's so gentle and sensitive," Golda offered weakly. She was worried herself about her son. Do you think it would be right if we visit them next week? She asked.

"I'm not sure. We'll see."

Pincas was in the store already getting busy when Adolph arrived looking like he was half asleep.

"What's the matter, son, you look awful." Pincas was concerned.

"I'm having some trouble at home, Papa. I'll tell you about it later." Pincas didn't answer. He went to the front door and sat down.

Suddenly Adolph came rushing over to his father. "Papa, she's coming. Please, hide somewhere. Please, I'll explain later. Go, Papa, I beg you, go."

Pincas was amazed, then alarmed. "What's the matter? What's going on?"

"Please, Papa, don't ask questions now, just hide somewhere. Hurry."

A bewildered man, Pincas hobbled to the back, not knowing where to go. He went into the lavatory and closed the door. He overheard Adolph saying, "See, he's not here." Then, some soft talking, which he couldn't make out, and then it was quiet.

Adolph was coming to the back of the store when Pincas slowly opened the lavatory door. He was ashen and stared at his son, waiting for an explanation. Adolph tried to say something, but couldn't make a sound. He put his arms around his father, and tears started to flow down his cheeks. Finally, he spoke.

"Papa, you can't imagine what I'm going through. She doesn't want you in the store. I told her that you put me in business, that we love working together with my brothers. She wants her family in the store. She says that they are poor and she has to do that for them. Papa, what can I do? It's hell for me from the time I get home until I get to sleep."

Pincas listened. He didn't answer. Slowly he limped to the front of the store and sat down. Adolph looked at his father. How sad he looked, his color drained from his face, his head down.

"Papa, talk to me. Tell me what to do. I'm miserable. You know, Papa, she's very nice to me, but she doesn't care how she hurts my family or me with the business. She says you are rich and can afford to open another business, and her family is poor and could never do that."

Pincas looked at his son. He is such a fine boy, he thought to himself, bright, but so weak and easily dominated. Why did I allow Mr. Finkelstein to arrange that meeting? If I hadn't, he would never have met her and he would be better off.

Aloud, he said, "I don't know what to say to you. I can't believe that a wife could dictate to her husband about his business. I'll have to talk to Mama." He put his head in his hands and rocked from side to side.

When Pincas came home, he opened the back door to a cheery hello, which became almost a shriek when Golda saw her husband's face. "What's the matter? What happened? Gut enu, please tell me, are the boys alright?" She was already twisting the hem of her apron.

"Golda, you will never believe what I'm about to tell you. Jean wants us to leave the business so her family can work there. Nu, did you ever hear of such a thing? She says we are rich and can open another store, but her family is poor and could never hope to do that."

Pincas also told her how he had to hide in the lavatory. Our son is miserable. Why can't he be a man and stand up to her is beyond me. But there it is, Golda. So what do we do now?"

Golda stood motionless. She was stunned.

"You are right, Pina. I can't believe it. What to do is a good question. I think maybe we should visit them. I'll bake a cake for good luck in their new home. We'll take the children and perhaps we'll straighten this mess out."

They dressed and made sure that the four children looked clean and neat. "Come, let's go," Pincas said as he went to the door. Nettie, Joey, Amy, and Millie went out and Golda followed. The children were very excited to go to their brother's apartment. They chattered and giggled all the way. They loved being on the train and had a very good time. Golda and Pincas were quiet and hardly spoke to each other. They were preoccupied in thought.

"Time to get off," said Pincas. They found the apartment building without any trouble and soon they were in front of the door.

"I'll knock," Pincas said with trepidation. When he did, it took a few minutes before Adolph opened the door.

"Mama, Pop, now you come? Why didn't you call?"

"Who is there?" It was Jean's voice.

"It's my mother and father, Jeannie," Adolph answered nervously.

Jean was at the kitchen table. She was wearing a housecoat and had her hair in a sort of nightcap. She looked at them with contempt in her eyes. Golda, with a package in her hand, was standing next to Pincas. The four children in front of them were uneasy.

They were just about to step into the apartment, when Jean blurted out, "Take your four pieces of shit and get out of my apartment. Adolph, get them out of here."

Adolph, shocked and shaken, looked from Jean to his parents and in utter despair cried out, "You'd better go, Mama and Papa. I'll come by the house and we'll talk, but for now, please leave."

After several attempts to find out what this outburst was about failed, and with Adolph's pleading for them to leave, they turned and walked out.

The following morning, after a sleepless night, Pincas told the boys everything that had happened, including the day that Jean had come into the store.

"Where were we when she came in?" asked Harry.

"You were both out, calling on trade," answered Pincas.

"I wish I had been there. I would have taken care of her," said Harry. "My brother is a wimp! No woman would get away with that with me."

"Harry, hold your tongue and your temper," cautioned Pincas. "Things are bad enough. We want to make things better, not worse."

Soon, Adolph appeared in the doorway of the kitchen. "Hello, I can only stay a few minutes, but I wanted to apologize for what happened. I'm so sorry. Listen, I'll help you get started in a new business. Oh, I feel so terrible."

"Adolph, I have to ask you a question. Is this the only thing that's upsetting your marriage?" Pincas was looking at his son, feeling sorry for him. He could see the pain and embarrassment on his face.

"Yes, Papa," Adolph answered. "She wants her family in the store."

"Go back to the business, Adolph," Pincas said, "we'll figure something out."

"Wait, let me fix a cup of coffee with something. You must be hungry. We'll all have some." Golda wanted to reinstate good feelings among the brothers, as well as having her son with her a little longer.

"I can't, Mama. Some other time real soon, I promise," answered Adolph. He hugged his mother and Father, waved to his brothers and was gone.

Harry watched his brother leave and said, "When I get married, if I ever do, I'll say to my wife, 'wash my mother's floor'."

Henry added quickly, "That's right, I will too."

"Stop it, boys. I can't stand this whole thing. Our family is being torn apart." Golda was so upset that she was walking back and forth in the kitchen wringing her hands.

"Golda, boys," Poppa said sternly. "Momma's right. We have a problem and somehow we will work it out."

A few days passed and Pincas called the boys and Golda together. "Come, sit down, I have a plan. We will open a small business. We'll sell silks, and rayons, instead of velvets, so as not to hurt Adolph. We'll make a living," Pincas spoke looking at Harry and Henry for approval.

"That's a good idea, and we can do it," Henry said and added, "I can't work in that store anymore knowing how Jean feels about us. But Papa, can we afford it?" Henry asked.

"We have a good name in the trade. We can take a loan and in no time we'll pay it back," Pincaas assured them.

"Papa, will you let us be known as **Pincas Meirowitz and Sons**?" asked Harry.

"No, for the same reason I told Adolph. You have to be open on Shabbos and I won't have my name on the window of a business that is open on Saturday. No matter," Pincas added quickly, "it will be **Harry Meirowitz and Brothers**. It will work out just fine."

While they were making plans and finding a store to rent, Henry was lining up the customers. He contacted manufacturers of dolls' dresses, umbrellas, coat linings, children's dresses, and cosmetic bags, and convinced them that he had beautiful plaid material. With their permission, he would bring them samples.

By the time that the store was open, Henry had gotten a fine start on orders. They were on the way to a good profiting business.

Adolph was doing very well. Jean's family worked in his business. Her brother became a salesman, her sister, Gilda, the secretary, her brother-in-law, Abe, worked in the store, and Jean's father sat in the front of the store as the watchman.

****

Things settled down, but Golda was very unhappy at the split in the family. "Pina," she said one evening as they sat alone in the kitchen sipping demitasse, "I can't stand not having Adolph for a Shabbos meal. We have to make shalom with Jean. Please call Adolph. Tell him to come to the store or here and we'll try to get our family together. Please Pina."

"Yes, you are right. I'll do that," Pina answered, but he really wasn't so confident that Jean would come to their home. The next morning Pincas called Adolph's business and was greeted by a friendly, "Good morning, Adolph Meirowitz, silks and velvets." Pincas was sure that voice belonged to Jean's sister, Gilda.

"Good morning, may I speak to Mr. Meirowitz? This is his father calling."

"Hello, Papa. How are you? And Mom? And everyone? Is everything, O.K.?"

Pincas sensed nervousness in his son's voice, but he ignored it and said, "Adolph, Mama and I would like you and Jean to come for Shabbos dinner. It's time we all got together."

Pincas was aware of the tense silence and he quickly added, "Adolph, talk to Jean before you answer me. Tell her we would be happy to have her and hold no grudges."

"O.K., Papa. I'll ask her. Good-bye, Papa."

It was about 4 P.M. when Adolph called his father. "Papa, she said, O.K. We'll come this Friday. Isn't that great?" Pincas heard the joy in Adolph's voice and it made him sad to think that Jean was in charge of his son's life. She made all the decisions.

"Mama will be so happy and so will the whole family," Pina said.

Everyone was happy except Harry. "Would you mind if I went to visit Bubba and Zaida? I don't want to see her," he said.

Golda was bringing the steaming platter of pot roast to the table and when she set it down she said, "Listen to me, all of you, especially you, Harry." She was really upset and began to twist a napkin from the table. "The whole family will be together for our Shabbos meal, all of you. You will behave properly. I'm not asking you to kiss Jean if you don't want to, but I insist that you be polite to her for your brother's sake and for Papa and me. Will you promise me that you'll be good?"

"I will," said little Millie. "I like Jeannie. Adolph told me that Jeannie eats carrots. That's why she had red cheeks. I'm gonna eat carrots, too, and so is Amy, right Amy?" Amy smiled and gave her sister a hug.

"Sure, Micky, sure."

Claire said, "Don't worry, Mom, everything will be fine. The boys don't want to hurt Adolph or you and Papa."

Golda prepared the Shabbos meal as usual, only this time she was very nervous. Did she put enough salt in the fish? Did it need a little more sugar? Was the chicken soup good? Was the meat tender? Will Jean like her kugel? Oh dear, she was sure her dinner would be a disaster.

Jean and Adolph arrived just as Golda was putting the finishing touches on the dinner. The house was spotless with the wonderful smells of the traditional Friday cooking; the glow from the Shabbos candles embraced them with a warm welcome.

"Gut Shabbos, children," Golda said. She was nervous not knowing what to do. Should she kiss her son and Jean? Should she wait for them to respond? She didn't have to wait long before Adolph gave her a tight hug and a kiss, and Jean leaned forward and offered her cheek.

"Come let's sit down. I'm so happy to see you." Golda was now a bit more relaxed and her face was glowing.

Dinner went well. The little children had a wonderful time. Jean was very attentive to them. She was also talkative to Adolph, whispering in his ear, which just delighted him. The brothers were quietly eating and spoke just to make an occasional comment on the good food.

"This fish is real good, Mom," said Henry. He didn't look at Jean or his brother.

"Have another piece, Henry," urged Golda.

"No thank you. I'm saving my appetite for the rest of the meal."

"Harry, would you please pass the horseradish to Adolph?" Golda was trying to get some interaction going between her sons, but Harry just passed the horseradish without looking at him or Jean. The rest of the meal went smoothly. The food was delicious and the girls kept pleasant conversation going. Harry and Henry went to their room, saying that they would be back soon. Adolph excused himself and followed his brothers.

"I know that you are angry with me and I'm sorry. I wish we could talk and perhaps you would understand my situation. I want our family to stay close. Harry, Henry, you know I would never hurt Mama or Papa, or any of you for that matter, but what can I do? I'm married and I have to make the best of it. Oh," he added quickly, "Jean is very nice to me and her family gives me the greatest respect. Please try to be pleasant to her, for my sake."

Harry was looking at his brother and didn't say anything for a while. Then he said, "How can I be pleasant to someone who threw my father out of his business? I don't care about us, Henry and I, but Papa? How could you have allowed that? If that's what a marriage is, I'll never get married."

After he said all that, he felt sorry. Poor Adolph, he thought, he's got enough trouble, I shouldn't add to it. He put his hands on Adolph's shoulder and said, "O.K., we'll try, right, Henry?" Henry nodded, and they went downstairs.

After that, Jean and Adolph came every Shabbos and that made Golda very happy.

****

Joe was an excellent student in high school. He was invited to join the Arista, which was a club for people who maintained an A average. Joe refused because he wanted to go to the Place. He would get there right after school, do his homework standing on one foot, the other bent, knee on a chair, close his books, and start working. He was helpful with cutting samples, making packages, answering the telephone. He loved being there.

"Joey," Golda would say to him often, "You should go to college. Your marks are so good; maybe you should be a doctor."

"No, Mama," he replied. "I want to be in the business. I can't wait to graduate so I can go to the Place every day.".

Harry Meirowitz and Brothers became a big business. They were respected in the garment section. They had the reputation of being honest and trustworthy, but wouldn't let anyone be late with a payment or take advantage. The boys and Pincas worked long and hard and got along very well together.

****

Jean became pregnant about four months after the wedding and Adolph was ecstatic. He called his parents and could hardly wait for them to say hello. "Mom, Papa," he announced, "Jean is going

106

to have a baby. I mean we are having a baby. Oh, can you believe it? I'm so excited, aren't you?"

"Mazel tov, dear boy, of course we're excited and just thrilled for you both. When is the baby due?" asked Golda.

"I'm not sure. I think in June. I'll let you know. Ma, tell the kids. Tell everybody," he said gaily.

"I will, I will," laughed Golda. "Calm down, Alteral. You will make a wonderful father. I know."

Aye, our first grandchild, thought Golda. I hope Jean will let us love and spoil baby. On the telephone she said, "When will you and Jean be here so we can congratulate you both in person?"

"I'm not sure, Mom. I'll let you know. Bye, Mama."

"Bye, my son," she answered as she slowly hung up the phone. He can't make a single decision by himself, she thought. I hope and pray it will get better when the baby comes.

Everyone was delighted with the news. "Micky, we are going to be aunts," said Amy. "Maybe Jean will let us hold the baby."

Millie was five years old and responded to everything that her sister said or did. "And maybe she'll let us wheel the carriage."

Even the boys were happy with the news.

Pincas was really finding it very difficult to get around. The brace seemed heavier these days, forcing him to have a severe limp and move much slower. He would have his dinner and then retire to his room so he could remove the brace. What a relief. Sometimes he would just sit on his chair, take a deep breath, and allow the burning sensation in his leg to subside. Golda would often come up to talk to him about the day's activities or ask about the goings-on in the Place.

"Pina, did you see or talk to Adolph today? I wonder how Jean is feeling these days. When they were here Friday evening, she was quite big and seemed a bit uncomfortable," Golda smiled remembering the feeling.

"It will be soon," Golda continued, "she looks like it will be a girl, she is round and her nose is a little broader, but you never know. Please, G- d, it should be a healthy baby and she should be well."

Pina smiled, too. "Well Golda, we are going to be grandparents, and I like that."

The following Friday morning, Adolph called to say that Jean was in labor and he was taking her to the hospital. Golda offered to go with them, but Adolph said no. He would keep them informed.

Constance Flora Meirowitz was born about noon and happier parents and grandparents couldn't be found.

"Mama, my daughter is the most beautiful child that I have ever seen. And Mama, she is so alert. Oh, Mama, I'm so happy."

"Of course you are, dear boy. When will we be able to see our granddaughter?"

"This afternoon. I'll pick you up."

The child was beautiful and, as Golda gazed at her, tears of joy rolled down her cheeks. She was so happy for Adolph. It was hard to realize that he was a father. He had been so sick as a little boy. They had feared for his life and now it all seemed like a dream.

Adolph was enjoying his mother's expression of happiness and love for his little daughter. "Mom, isn't she the most perfect baby that you have ever seen?"

Golda laughed. "Sweetheart, she's just gorgeous. I can't wait for Papa to see her. Our first grandchild! Someday, with G-d's help, you and Jean will know how it feels to be grandparents. When can I see Jean?"

"As soon as we leave the nursery, we'll go to her room."

Jean looked lovely in her new nightgown and matching robe. Golda noticed that she had a red ribbon tucked in her gown. Jean was superstitious and the red ribbon was to ward off an evil eye.

"Mazel tov, Jean. Thank you for making Papa and me grandparents. The baby is darling! May you raise her in good health."

"Thank you. Did Adolph tell you her name is Constance Flora?"

"Yes, he did and I think it's a beautiful name."

"Well, son, if you don't mind, I'd like to go home. I must prepare dinner. Adolph, please come eat with us while Jean is in the hospital."

"O.K. Mom. Thanks and let's go." He bent to kiss Jean goodbye and said, "Jeannie, I'm going to stop and get cigars, see how everything is at the store, and come back. Kiss Connie for me when you nurse her."

Oh, Golda thought, my son is crazy with joy. Please G-d, may they all be well and happy. To Jean she said, "Be a healthy and happy mother. We'll see you soon."

To Jean and Adolph's delight the baby thrived. She was a happy, alert, and active child. The family loved her especially Amy and Millie. They came quite often. Golda and Pincas only went to visit them when they were invited. They didn't see Jean's family much.

****

Pincas and Golda returned from the doctor's office tired and pensive. "Pina, is a cataract operation dangerous? How long will you be in the hospital? Pina, do you realize that this is the first time we will be separated?"

"Goldala, Goldala, don't worry. I'll be fine. It is a good excuse to rest my foot. Really, it is a common operation. I'll be O.K."

For Golda, it wasn't easy. She walked to the Israel Zion Hospital, and when she got there she was not allowed in because the visiting hours were from one to four and then from six to eight. She hadn't asked about visiting hours. Having no experience with hospitals, she took it for granted that she could see her husband anytime.

Golda sat on the steps until they let her in. Her heart was pounding as she approached the bed where he was lying very still. His head was rigid in sort of a box, his eyes bandaged. Golda was frightened. "Pina," she whispered, "can you hear me?"

"Yes, Goldala, I can hear you. I'll be all right. The doctor said it went well, so don't worry."

"Oh, Pina. It's so lonely without you. Are you eating? Do they help you with meals?" she asked him as she stroked his arm.

"Yes, they are very kind to me. They feed me. I'm not very hungry these days. Of course, if it were your cooking, I would eat much more. I miss you too. How are the children? Everyone O.K.? Please G-d, they will take the bandage off soon and then I'll be able to go home."

"Everyone is fine and can't wait for you to come home," answered Golda.

When Pincas came home, the family was very happy and doted on him. "Papa, what can we do for your?" Amy and Millie asked as they hugged and kissed him.

"Oh mine tira kindelach (*my dear children*), I'm fine. Now that I'm home, I have everything."

****

In a few weeks Pincas was back in the Place, and life resumed as usual. Pincas was approached by fathers and matchmakers. "Mr. Meirowitz," they would say, "I have a wonderful girl for your son Harry."

Harry was a desirable man. He had a very good name in his thriving business, came from a fine family and was a handsome young man. What more could a father want for his daughter? Some promised dowries of money, others a house, all had the ideal girl for Harry.

When Pincas told Harry to call on one of these young ladies, Harry said, "Papa, what's wrong with her? She must be big and fat, or have a wooden leg or something. I really don't want to call."

"Harry," Papa persisted, "call her, what have you got to lose?"

"O.K. Papa, I'll call, but if I don't like her, that's it, right?"

"Absolutely, son." Pincas was glad that Harry consented to call. Harry was different from Adolph. He was a most considerate son, caring and protective of his family, adoring to his mother, but he was a strong-willed man, one that couldn't be pushed around.

"Golda, Harry called that young lady and made a date with her," Pincas said. "They are Hungarian. Well, at least they aren't Galitzioners, or tailors." Pincas said. "May G-d protect my children from tailors or Galitzioners in marriage."

"Pina," Golda said, "your son married a Romanian, and see how that is. We are in America, and all people should be accepted."

"Well, I just hope they don't marry tailors or Galitzioners," he said stubbornly. Golda smiled as she shook her head.

Harry seemed to like this girl and one morning at breakfast he asked his mother if he could invite Hannah for dinner.

"Of course, Harry, bring her for Shabbos dinner. We would love to meet her."

"Mom, now don't get excited. I'm not sure yet. I'm not jumping in so fast."

"Whatever you say, Hershala." Golda smiled and thought, this boy is in love, but he won't give in so quickly. To him she said, "What does she look like?"

Harry thought for a minute and then answered, "She's cute. She has beautiful hair. It's shiny and sort of brown with some red in it. She's pretty and smart. Well, I don't know. We'll see."

Hannah came and Harry's description of her was exactly as he said. She was a lovely girl as well, and Harry was so pleased to see that she fit right in with the family.

Mr. and Mrs. Rosenblatt invited Golda and Pincas to dinner at their home. They had a beautiful apartment in Manhattan. They were obviously wealthy people, however, they were not boastful. They were very hospitable and respectful. A maid served the dinner that was elegant. Oh vey, Golda thought, how will they feel in our simple house? What will I serve them?

They accepted Harry warmly and the evening ended in a friendly, we must together again soon, manner.

"Pina, did you notice the china, the tablecloth, the silver?" asked Golda when they were home getting ready for bed.

Pincas knew what his wife was thinking about and he said, "They do have a beautiful home. They are fine people and that's the important thing."

He put his arms around her. "Don't worry. When they come here, taste your food, and see our lovely family, they will be proud to have their daughter marry Harry. Hannah is a darling girl and I think it is a good match."

****

Harry and Hannah were in a coffee shop for some refreshments after an enjoyable movie.

"Hannah," he said," I have to talk to you about something very important.

"What is it, Harry?" Her eyes were shining with excitement and expectancy.

"I want to propose to you, ask you to marry me, but I have to be sure of one thing." He continued not waiting for a response from her. "I will not interfere with the household. That will be your responsibility unless you ask me. But you will not tell me how to run my business, who I should hire or fire."

He looked at her. She was beautiful and he loved her, but he would walk right out of her life if she didn't agree to that. He wouldn't allow anyone to hurt his father or brothers again.

"Oh Harry, I would never do that. I care a lot for your family and I'm sure I'll love them when I get to know them better. I would never want to do anything that would come between you and your family. I would never hurt you like that."

"I was sure you would say that! So, Hannah, will you marry me?"

Harry cupped her face in his hand, smiled, and kissed her gently on the lips. She blushed with a bit of embarrassment to be kissed in a restaurant among people.

"Yes, Harry," she said tenderly. "I will marry you and be a good wife."

They had a beautiful wedding at the Chelsea Hotel on Fifth Avenue, went on a short honeymoon, and Hannah became part of the family.

****

"Amy, wouldn't you like to be a Girl Scout?" Hannah asked.

"They have a lot of fun. Find out where there is a troop and see if you would like it. I'll buy the outfit for you."

"Thank you, Hannah. I know where they meet and I know some of the girls. I would love to join." Amy was delighted.

"Well Micky, how do I look?" asked Amy as she stood dressed her Girl Scout uniform.

"Just beautiful, Amy. Someday, I'll be a Girl Scout, too," said Millie a bit wistfully. They did almost everything together, but she was too young to be a Girl Scout.

Hannah proved to be a loving and dutiful wife to Harry and a devoted and caring daughter-in-law to Pina and Golda. She was a delightful addition to the family.

Millie came home from school one day and told Amy that she didn't feel well. Her jaw hurt and she could hardly open her mouth without a great deal of pain.

"A bath is what you need to make you feel better," Amy said with authority. She knew whenever Mama had a headache, Nettie would say, "Mama, you need to take a nice bath to relax. I'll fill the tub."

As Millie sat in the tub, Amy noticed that her cheek was quite swollen. "I'd better tell Mama."

When Golda saw Millie's face, she immediately said, "Malkala, get out of the tub right now. I think that you have the mumps."

Hannah sent two books to Millie, *Hans Brinker and the Silver Skates* and *A Child's Garden of Verses,* by Robert Louis Stevenson. They were beautifully illustrated and were inscribed. One said, To Millie: Hurry up and get well, and the other said: "Nobody loves a sick girl. Get well quickly."

Two weeks later Amy came down with the mumps, a mild case, and soon it was all forgotten.

****

Amy was twelve when she starting menstruating. She knew how to take care of herself from her friends. Her friend Laura had given her two Kotex pads and now she needed to buy some. She asked her mother for some money for the purchase. Golda saw the embarrassment on Amy's face.

"Amyalla, don't be ashamed, be proud. You are growing up. I'm the one that should be ashamed. I should have told you about it, not your friends. Somehow I didn't think it would happen so soon. Forgive me, my little woman." She hugged her daughter and then gave her money.

Amy and Millie were walking and came upon the drug store. "Micky," Amy said. "Go in and ask for a box of Kotex."

"What's that?" asked Millie.

"Never mind. Just go in and ask. Here's the money," said Amy as she steered her sister to the door and pushed her through.

Standing in the store and being sure it was something secretive, she became embarrassed and almost whispered, "A box of Kotex, please."

"Why do you always make me go into the store for you? What's that for anyway?" Millie asked.

"I'll tell you someday," Amy answered as she smiled and patted her little sister's head.

"Remember, don't tell anyone that we bought Kotex. It's nobody's business." Amy was a very private person, and would always caution Millie not to mention certain things to their friends.

****

Golda was serving tea to her neighbor Sophie, who was also from Romania. It was Saturday afternoon and they were having a lovely time talking about the old days, people from their little village, when Sophie remarked, "Golda, do you remember Katrinka?"

Golda thought for a minute. "Yes," she said. "She used to work for the Epsteins, right? I remember she hardly had a nose, just nostrils. What about her?"

"Well," said Sophie, "she came to America with the Epsteins. Mr. Epstein passed away and Mrs. Epstein is going to a home. Katrinka has no place to go. No family. No home. It's such a pity."

Golda hardly took a moment to reply. "I'll take her in. I could use a little help in the house. My children are growing up so fast. Thank G-d. Claire will marry soon, and the girls are busy with school. It would be nice for Katrinka and me. Do you know how to get in touch with her?"

Sophie looked at Golda. "I knew you would say that. You are so good, pretending you need help in order to make the girl feel welcome. I'll tell her to come and see you. O.K.?"

A few days later, Katrinka came to the back door of the house and timidly knocked.

"I'm coming," responded Golda. She recognized Katrinka immediately and welcomed here warmly.

"Come in, we'll have a cup of coffee with something and we'll talk."

"Thank you, Mrs. Meirowitz; I didn't take the time to eat this morning."

Poor girl, thought Golda, she must be half-starved. And her heart hurt for her. "I haven't had breakfast either, so we'll eat together. I made oatmeal for the family this morning and there is some left so you can have it, O.K.?"

Golda noticed how eagerly Katrinka devoured the bread and butter, cleaned the bowl of oatmeal, and enjoyed the coffee.

"Katrinka," Golda said, "would you like to stay with us for a while? I could use some help in the house. I think you would be happy here. If it works out well, you could stay as long as you like."

"Oh thank you, Mrs. Meirowitz, I would love to. I'll do anything you tell me to. I have an aunt living in America, but I don't know where she lives and can't get in touch with her."

Golda warned the children not to laugh or stare at Katrinka's nose, to be kind to her and make her feel welcome. Katrinka became part of the household and was a great help to Golda. She stayed with them for eight years. She left to live with the aunt who eventually found her and wanted Katrina to live with her own family. There were hugs, kisses, and tears from the children and Katrinka when she left.

****

Golda was putting the last dish away when Pincas sat down with the newspaper.

"Pina," she said, "Do you realize how beautiful Nettie has become? I worry about her. I'll be happy when she meets the right boy and marries. She'll be the perfect wife and mother."

Nettie loved clothes and was always dressed beautifully. She had good taste and was a good shopper. She would nag Golda to call Adolph for an invitation to some of the showrooms of the dress manufacturers who bought his silks and velvets. He would never refuse his mother and always paid for the dresses, urging her to pick out more.

Nettie was also a wonderful homemaker. She helped Golda with the housework, with the cooking and baking and was happy staying home. She didn't even look for a job and Golda did not urge her to. She loved having her home.

"Golda, you always worry about something," Pincas answered with affection. "If it's not the children, you worry about me. Please stop worrying. Everything will be all right. You'll see.

Golda did worry about her children, especially her daughters, knowing each one very well. Claire was very intelligent, very outspoken, an achiever. Nettie was soft-spoken, gentle, and definitely a potential homemaker. Amy was very studious, dependable and caring for the family, especially for her little sister. And Millie, the youngest, was a dreamer.

Millie loved babies and her hobby was collecting baby pictures. She had many albums of beautiful babies with original, hand written captions under each picture. She also loved to design hairdos. She would sit and watch her sister Claire dress for a date and imagine her with an exotic hairstyle. When she went out dancing in a lovely Grecian style chiffon dress, Millie envisioned her wearing a beautiful Grecian wig. She was excited and determined to make wigs for stylish women.

****

"Mamma, when I grow up would you open a salon for me on Fifth Avenue to design wigs?" Millie wistfully asked. Golda was sitting on a rocking chair on the porch knitting. She looked up from her work and stared at her daughter.

"What?" she exclaimed, "sheitels" (*wigs*) you want to make, are you mishiga (*crazy*)?"

"No Mamma. I'm not crazy. Women wear all kinds of different styles of clothing. They should have a special hairdo to match their outfit. I would make a suitable wig. I would wash it and set it for them. It would be a good business, I'm sure."

Golda laughed. "Don't be silly. Do your homework. Get good marks. That's more important for you than to think about than making wigs. Maybe you'll be a teacher like your Aunt Helen, or a bookkeeper, or even a stenographer like your sister Claire."

"Wigs! Of all things." Golda chuckled again. "Go min kind, go do your schoolwork."

Millie left the porch and went to the room she and Amy shared. It wasn't very large, but it was comfortable for them. Amy was sitting at her desk working.

"Hi Mickey. Finish your homework. If you need any help, just ask me."

Amy noticed that her sister looked sad. "What's the matter Mick?"

"Nothing. I guess I'll never do what I want".

"What do you want?" asked Amy.

"Mamma says I'm crazy, but I to want to make wigs. Maybe I am, but I still want to."

Amy put her arms around her sister, "Listen, first you have to grow up, and then you'll see. You might change your mind, you don't know. Come on finish your homework and we'll read in bed O.K.?"

They always read in bed until Golda would come in and make them put out the lights and go to sleep.

****

"Micky, let's go. Laura and her sister are walking towards our house and we'll meet them. Come on."

Millie answered in a frightened way, "I can't go. Something happened to me, I'm sick."

"What hurts you?" Amy became alarmed. She hurried to the bathroom and found her sister pale and nervous.

"What's the matter Micky?" Amy asked softly. Millie held out her panties, which had a brownish red stain on them.

"Something terrible is wrong with me. Oh I'm so scared. I'm afraid to tell Mamma. She'll take me to the doctor and they'll put me in the hospital."

Amy laughed with great relief, "Oh you dummy you have your period. You are growing up so fast. I'll show you what to do and you don't have to tell Laura and her sister. Just tell Mamma. You'll get this every month so don't get scared."

Millie was listening intently to everything her sister was saying. "You call it a period? All girls get it? You get it too Amy? How come you never told me?"

"Of course I get it. Remember when you went into that store to buy Kotex? Well that's what you have to wear when this happens. Wait I'll bring one in and show you how to use it. And remember don't tell anyone. Also Micky, I noticed you have a little hair under your arms. I'll take it off like I do mine. Don't worry I'll take care of you."

"Amy, you are my best friend and my best sister. I love you."

"I love you too. I'll be right back". She returned with the Kotex pad and showed Millie how to put it on. "There you are. Now Micky, you have to forget it and go about your business. So let's meet Laura and Mildred."

These two girls were sisters, close in age and very devoted. They accepted Millie even though she was so much younger. They would go for walks, usually to 13th Avenue, where they would buy a hot dog at Skilowitz, the best and most popular deli in the area. They ate as they continued to walk. They talked about books, movies, school, and family. Laura and Mildred had no brothers or sisters and they loved to listen to Amy and Millie tell of family activities.

"You are so lucky to have a large family," Laura would often remark.

"You have so much fun and there is always something going on," Mildred would add.

"That's true," said Millie. "Our sister Claire is getting married."

And Amy chimed in, "and Hannah is going to have a baby."

"That sure is exciting," said Laura. "Well I think we should go home. See you tomorrow."

The girls waved good-bye and went home.

****

Harry was worried about Hannah. "Please be careful Hannah. Don't lift anything heavy. Walk slowly, drink milk, and eat good food. I'll do whatever has to be done when I get home from work. Please, I don't want you to strain yourself. I want my child to have a healthy mother."

Hannah looked at him and smiled. "Harry do you think I'm the first woman to have a baby? Don't worry. The doctor says I'm fine and so is the baby. I wonder what it is- a boy or a girl. Do you care Harry?"

"Of course not, I just want you and the baby to be well. I hope it looks just like you," Harry said softly as he kissed her cheek.

The months passed and Hannah gave birth to a fine boy. The birth was a difficult one and the doctor advised her not to have any more children. Harry was ecstatic with his son. This beautiful child was his and Hannah's. He couldn't believe it.

"Did you ever see such a baby? Such perfect features. Thank you dear Hannah for our son. You must rest now. You had a rough time"

Hannah smiled, "It was worth it Harry. When I look at him and see how darling he is, and I see your happiness. I feel so good."

Golda, Pincas, and the Rosenblatts celebrated this blessed event at the Bris (*circumcision*) and were so happy with their grandson. The baby was named Martin.

Harry was very nervous about the Bris. He had never been to one before. He knew what it was and what had to be done but to his son. He was ashamed to let anyone know how he felt, but he worried. Poor little kid he thought. I hope it doesn't hurt him. I hope that the Moyel (*the clergy who performs the circumcision*) knows what he's doing. Gosh, I wish it were over....

Golda sensed what he was going through and she gently put her arm around him. "Harry," she said softly. "Don't worry. The baby will be fine. He's your son. He's strong like his father."

Harry responded with a smile and embraced his mother. "Oh Mamma, you always say the right thing. My son, boy does that sound good. Isn't he the most beautiful baby you've ever seen?"

Golda jokingly answered, "Of course, that's because he's my grandson, my first grandson.

The ceremony began. Pincas took his place as sondick. *(The sondick, usually a grandfather of the baby, is given the honor of holding the baby's legs as the Moyel performs the circumcision.)* As he held his grandson, tears of joy rolled down his cheeks.

"Mazel Tov, Mazel Tov!" everyone said.

Little Martin was sleeping after the few dabs of wine were dabbed on his little mouth. Harry was so proud and happy and gave everyone he saw a cigar.

Hannah was a born mother. She had a nana for the baby, but she was entirely involved with little Martin. They were a very happy family.

****

"Mamma, Poppa, I have something to tell you", exclaimed Nettie. "When Ben said good night to me he told me that he loves me. He wants to marry me. He asked me how I felt about him. I was ashamed to say I love him too, so I told him to please call me tomorrow and then I ran in the house. Oh can you imagine? He loves me."

Golda looked at her beautiful daughter and thought how sweet and gentle she is and now absolutely radiant she looks right now. "Mine tira kind (*my dear child*), why shouldn't he love you? You are a wonderful girl, beautiful, bright. Alla mallas," she said as she embraced her.

"He's a fine fellow even if he is a Glitziana, chimed in Pina.

"You can become engaged after Claire's wedding. Oh Pina, our children are leaving the nest so quickly." Golda was smiling as she said that, but there was a twinge of sadness on her face.

Pincas looked at his wife. She is still beautiful, he thought, a little heavier and a few wisps of gray in her curly hair but beautiful and gentle. "Golda, that's the way life is. Thank G-d our girls found fine boys. I hope the others will do the same in due time."

"Nettie, tell Ben that we like him, and that as soon as your sister's wedding is over we would like to meet his family. Is that all right with you?"

"Oh yes, thank you Momma and Poppa. You are the best parents in the whole wide world." Nettie was jumping up and down and hugging Golda and Pincas. "Oh I'm so happy."

****

Preparations for Claire's wedding were all settled. Claire found the place where she wished to be married. It was called Carfines and was a small but very nice place. Everyone was very happy.

Al was a fine man and the family loved him. The boys became very close and were like brothers. Al started a small business selling gas appliances. He had a franchise with the Brooklyn Union Gas Company. Claire worked in the store as a salesperson and was the bookkeeper as well. She would make appointments for plumbing jobs. They worked very hard and made a modest living.

"Millie," said Golda, "please dear, go to Claire's store after school. She is so tired. She needs to rest a little before she makes supper for Al."

Millie looked so hurt. "Momma, I'm supposed to play basketball after school. You know that. I asked for your permission to stay later, and Mrs.

Ostroff says they need me on the team. Oh, why do I have to go there? It's so boring."

Golda looked at the sad face on her youngest child. It really wasn't fair to make the child give up her basketball, but Claire was so tired. Golda put her arms around Millie and said softly, "I know how you feel Malkala, but your big sister needs you. A family has to help each other. You'll play ball another day."

She kissed her daughter and said gently, "You are so good. I know you'll go and help Claire."

Millie went the next day and then every afternoon after school. She gave up playing ball. Very few people came into the store to look at gas stoves or water heaters. It was very boring.

One afternoon a man came into the store with a tzedukah box (*charity box*). The man spoke Yiddish and asked Millie for a donation. She was so delighted that she could converse in the Yiddish language.

"How much does one have to give?" she asked in perfect Yiddish.

The man eyed her and said, "a quarter."

Millie had a pencil box with a zipper around it. She knew she had seven cents in it. She was given fifteen cents a day to buy a drink and some candy at lunchtime. Mamma made a sandwich for her. Poppa said you had to save a little for charity. She would always put her change in the tzedukah box at home.

She wanted to prolong the man's stay in the store, so she said, "I don't have a quarter."

"Then give me ten cents," he said a bit impatiently.

"I don't have ten cents. I have only seven cents," she answered.

"Gey in derate (*go to hell*). Give me the seven cents!" he yelled out to her.

She quickly unzipped her pencil box and fearfully gave him the money. He grabbed the money and left the store muttering words that Millie didn't understand.

When she came home, she cried and told Golda the story. "I'm never going to save my money to give to charity. He was so mean and he scared me. I should have spent all my money on candy then I could have brought home more for you."

Millie made it a habit of bringing home most of the candy she bought to her mother because Golda loved penny candy.

Now Golda smiled. Looking at her daughter's tear stained face she said, "Mommala, this is plenty for me. Thank you. Please stop crying. You did the right thing and I'm very proud of you. So will Poppa when you tell him."

Pincas listened intently to Millie's story and then drew her to him. He stroked her red gold hair and said very gently, "Malkala, just because one person is a fool and doesn't know how to talk to a beautiful, intelligent girl, is no reason to stop doing the right thing. We must share with the needy. I'm proud of you, too."

Millie left the room appeased and even a bit happy. She wanted her parents to be proud of her.

"It's not that they don't like me," she confided to Amy. "It's like my things aren't important and everyone else's are. Amy, I love them so much, and sometimes I feel that I'm nothing."

"Don't be ridiculous. What a thing to say." Amy put her arms around her sister and gave her a tight squeeze.

"Momma and Poppa love you and everyone in this family. Poor Momma. She works so hard, always worries about everyone, and never complains. Micky, please don't ever say or even think that again. And to me, you are my most favorite sister and friend."

Millie looked at her and said softly, "I know, and I'm sorry I said all those things. I know Momma is worried about Claire. I heard her tell Poppa that she wants to take her to the doctor."

Amy still had her arms around her little sister. "Don't worry," she said. "Claire will be fine. Come on lets finish our homework and then we'll help Momma."

Amy was a hard worker. No matter what she did, she did thoroughly. Her schoolwork was very good. She was always prompt with her assignments. Her teachers were delighted to have Amy as their student.

****

"Come in Mrs. Meirowitz. Come in. How are you and how can I help you?" Dr. Miriam was standing in his office with his two hands outstretched. He was a very pleasant looking man with blond red hair, blue eyes, and a gentle smile.

"Good afternoon doctor," Golda said warmly as she quickly took his hands in hers.

With a deep breath she said, "Doctor, I'm so worried about Claire. She wants a baby so badly. She cries so much, especially now that Nettie is pregnant. You said you would call her after the results from the tests were in and I was afraid to ask her if you had called."

"No, Mrs. Meirowitz, I just found out about the results. I'll call her later. There is nothing wrong with either one of them, but there is a problem. You see, Claire's womb is high and Al's sperm is weak and cannot reach the womb. That's why she can't conceive. Do you understand Mrs. Meirowitz?"

Golda's face was red with embarrassment. Oy vey, she thought. To talk to a man about things like that. I don't know what he's talking about. The mid wife took care of me and that was that. Gut e nu, my poor daughter. I don't know what's wrong with her.

To the doctor she said, "Should I tell Claire to come to see you?"

Dr. Miriam smiled noticing how frustrated Golda was and answered politely, "There is nothing to do .Of course she can call me anytime. Tell her to relax and try not to think about it so much. Sometimes that helps. Good afternoon Mrs. Meirowitz."

"Good afternoon Dr. Miriam," answered Golda, and she left the office. She decided not to tell Claire that she had been to the doctor's office in order to avoid any more talk about her condition. G-d will take care of Claire prayed Golda.

****

Saturday mornings always found Amy and Millie in bed reading and munching rugalach. Millie would tiptoe down to the kitchen and take some rugalach from the covered tray, wrap them in a napkin and hurry up to bed. They would hide them under the bed sheet, where they would nibble and read. Golda didn't allow any eating in the bedrooms, especially in bed, unless someone was sick.

"Millie," said Golda, "Claire just called. She asked me to please send you over to stay in her store so that she could rest a little. She told me to tell you that she made chocolate pudding for you. So you'll go, yes?"

"Oh Mom, do I have to? Why can't I stay home? I love Saturday mornings at home. Gosh I hate to go there. I think I'll stay home. O K?"

Golda knew it was unfair, but she also knew that Claire was tired and unhappy at this time in her life. "Do whatever you think, but please call her if you are not going over."

"I'll call her," Millie replied, and promptly dialed the number. "Hello, it's me." But before she could say one word, Claire was talking.

"Millie? Oh I need you to come and stay in the store for a few hours. You are such a dear. I'm so tired and I made chocolate pudding for us, just you and me. Oh I can't wait to see you."

Millie was going to tell her that she wasn't coming, but couldn't say that now. She is my oldest sister, she thought. I do feel sorry for her, even though I don't know what's wrong. She seemed so very sad. "OK, I'll be over soon."

"Well, I'm going. I just couldn't refuse," announced Millie to Amy as she entered the bedroom. Golda was gone and Amy was already making the bed.

"How come you never go Amy? Mom never asks you?"

Amy looked at her sister. Poor kid, she thought. It's true. They know that I wouldn't go. Aloud she said, "I'm too busy, homework and you know I help in the house. But Micky, you don't have to go all the time. You are too good and Claire knows that you won't say no to her."

"That's what I meant the other day when I said that I felt so unloved, sort of like pushed around," replied Millie.

"Nonsense, that's not so at all. Mom really believes that families must do for each other. Since you are the youngest and have less responsibility, it's alright for you to go. You really shouldn't build this up in your mind. When you come home we'll have some fun, OK?"

"OK," Millie sighed. She dressed and left for the store. Claire and Al's store was on the ground floor and their apartment was above it.

"Oh Millie darling, I'm so glad to see you," said Claire, as she gathered her book keeping things together and started for the door.

"You'll close the store at twelve o'clock and come up to my apartment. We'll have chocolate pudding, O.K honey? Call me if you need me."

Millie nodded and settled herself at the desk and opened her book. The time went so slowly. Not one person called or came into the store. Finally, it was time to close. Millie locked up and went to the apartment.

It was a charming three room flat with a kitchen, bedroom, living room, and a nice foyer. It was sunny and immaculate. The furniture was sparse but sturdy. Lovely sheer curtains on the windows and a nice rug on the floor made it homey and inviting.

"Come Millie, the pudding is on the table already. You'll love it."

Millie smiled. Her big sister was sweet. It really was too bad that she was so unhappy because she didn't have a baby. What's wrong with her anyway?

Aloud she said, "Claire, why can't you have a baby? How does a woman get pregnant? How does the baby get into her stomach?"

Claire was astonished at the lack of sex education this child had. "Don't you know? Didn't Amy ever tell you? Or Momma? Didn't you ever read about reproduction in a book? I can't believe it!" exclaimed Claire in bewilderment.

"Well I'll tell you." She stood up and slowly walked across the kitchen floor.

"You see when a man and a woman marry they are in love with one another. They are intimate. The husband plants a seed in his wife's body and it grows into a baby. It's beautiful and wonderful, and...," at that point Claire started to cry.

Millie sat very quietly. She was sorry she made her sister cry, but she still persisted. "How does he plant the seed?" she asked.

Claire tried to explain noticing how shocked and frightened Millie appeared. "Being married and having a family is the most natural and wonderful thing Millie. Don't be so upset," she said gently.

Millie jumped up from her chair and ran to the bathroom where she threw up. She rinsed her mouth and then stated that she was going home.

How could Momma and Poppa do such a thing? And her brothers Adolph, Harry, and sister Nettie, how could they? She remembered she had seen dogs in the street stuck together yelping. Oh how awful she thought.

When she came into the house, it was quiet. Saturday afternoon Momma and Poppa rested if there was no company. She found Amy reading and her first impulse was to ask her why she didn't tell her. Maybe she doesn't know Millie thought, and decided not to mention it to her.

"Hi Mick, glad you're home. Was the pudding good?"

Millie nodded and asked, "Are Momma and Poppa sleeping?"

"I guess so. They always take a nap on Shabbos, why?"

"Nothing, I was just wondering," answered Millie, "want to go for a walk?"

"Sure, "answered Amy, puzzled at the way Millie looked and spoke, "Are you O.K.? Anything wrong?"

"No, let's go," Millie was already walking out the door.

"Maybe Laura and Mildred can come too," said Amy. "I'll call them. I'll just be a minute."

Millie decided to not to talk about her terrible experience but secretly resolved never to marry and have children.

****

Pincas was finding it more painful to walk and do the things around the house he used to do. He found it difficult to go to the synagogue on the Sabbath, and he often had to stop and rest on his cane or lean against a tree on the way. Golda noticed how tired and strained he looked as he came into the house.

He sat down with a sigh of relief. "Good Shabbos my dear Golda. It's so wonderful to be home. The sermon was excellent, and I was given an honor," he said proudly.

"Good Shabbos Pina. I'm happy you enjoyed shul, but you look so tired. I know you are in pain. I'll serve lunch and then you'll take off that brace and rest."

She served him a little glass of wine and a piece of honey cake. As she placed it before him she stroked his face. "Poor man, how I wish I could take the pain away," she said sadly.

Pincas grabbed her hand and kissed it. "Goldala, Goldala, what would I do without you? You have made my life so worthwhile. You have given me such wonderful children, a beautiful home, and you are so good and kind to me. I'm so lucky," he said. "I thank the good Lord for my blessings every day."

"Me too," said Golda earnestly. "And speaking of the children, Henry goes out with a different girl every week judging from the color of the lipstick on his handkerchiefs." She laughed. "He sure is one handsome boy. I don't blame the girls."

Pincas laughed too. Those boys are really something. "I like Joey's friend, Anthony, the Italian boy. What a fine young man," said Pincas. "These two boys respect each other's holidays, date girls of their own faith. It's very nice."

"That's true." Golda was bringing a steaming bowl of chicken soup with matzo balls to the table. As she placed it before him she said, "Joey goes with one girl. Her name is Ethel. I think they are a family of five girls and one boy. They have no father. The mother is in the real estate business."

Pincas gazed at his wife and laughed. "How come you know so much about this girl and her family?"

"Well, I like to know who my children are going out with and I ask," replied Golda.

The soup was followed by chicken, noodle pudding, and compote (*a mixture of stewed prunes, dried apricots, and pears*). This was a typical Saturday after shul meal. Usually the girls, Amy and Millie, would have lunch with them, but this weekend they were invited to Jean and Adolph's home to play with Connie.

As Golda cleared the table she said, "I hope the girls enjoy the baby and everything will be alright."

"There you go again, always worrying. Come on, what could go wrong?" asked Pincas.

"Well," said Golda slowly, "you know Jean. She can be so bossy. And Amy and Millie are sensitive, especially Millie."

Pincas was slowly stirring his tea and moved his head from side to side.

She continued, "Why is Adolph so afraid of her? He doesn't have a mind of his own. Every time he opens his mouth he looks to her for approval. Our boys call him a wimp. I don't know exactly what that means, but I think it means that he's weak and has nothing to say. Thank G-d he has that baby. She's his life."

"Golda, he loves his business and he's becoming a rich man. Thank the good Lord."

"But she insists on having her family work there. They all make a good living from the Place—her brother, brother- in-law, her sister, and her father all do very well. I really don't care about that. If only he wasn't so scared of her and could have some things his own way."

"Well, there is nothing we can do. Just hope for the best." Pincas said. However, silently he agreed and wished things were different for this son.

"Finish your tea," Golda sighed, "and then go take your shoe and brace off and rest. I don't expect anyone this afternoon."

She pondered Adolph a bit longer as she tidied up the kitchen, wishing all the while that his situation with Jean were better.

****

The girls returned home Sunday afternoon. They traveled by train and loved the ride.

"Well, tell me all about your visit. How is Connie? What did you do with her? How are Jean and Adolph? Did you have a good time?" Golda was anxious to hear that all was well with her son and his wife.

When they came on Fridays for dinner it always was a bit tense. She tried to make sure that the boys wouldn't say anything to Jean that would be in any way upsetting. They were cordial but distant. They couldn't forget or forgive her for what happened at the Place.

"Connie is beautiful and lots of fun," answered Millie. "And do you know what? I taught her to do the Varsity Drag. She did it very well, right Amy?"

"Yes, and we had a good time except at dinner on Friday," replied Amy.

"Oh it was awful," Millie chimed in. "Jean's mother cooked cabbage soup. Mom, you know we don't like that soup, and we weren't going to eat it. Adolph came over to us and whispered that we had better eat it and to say it was delicious or we would be sorry."

"Uch," grimaced Amy. "It was terrible. We hated it, but we ate it."

Momma, why is Adolph so afraid of Jean?" asked Millie. "He gave us both five dollars and told us not to say anything to Jean."

Golda listened and tried not to show her feelings. Her sweet son, to be so tense and to live in fear of his wife. He is such a fine man, handsome and rich. He gives her everything she wants and takes care of her family. They all make a living from his business. It really hurt her.

Aloud she said, "He just wants everything to go smoothly and everyone to be happy. Are you hungry?" she asked not wanting to continue this discussion.

"Take some milk and have some cookies. I just baked them this morning. Please clean up when you finish," she said as she left the kitchen. She went to talk to her husband.

"There is nothing we can do," said Pincas sadly, when Golda related the children's account of their visit. "We can help him if we stay out of things that might upset Jean. We must not find fault or tell Adolph what we think he should do. We will always make them welcome at our home, but we will not visit them without an invitation. Golda, I think he loves her. We know he adores Connie, so he is happy. Let's not bother him and he'll be all right." Pincas was trying to sooth his unhappy wife.

"You are so smart Pina. You always say the right thing to make me feel better," said Golda as she planted a kiss on his cheek.

Things were going along fairly well for Golda and Pincas and the family. Harry's business was very lucrative and the boys and Pincas were happy at the Place.

Nettie had a beautiful baby and was so happy with him and with her husband Ben. He was a fine man who loved the family and was always ready to be helpful if needed. He worked for a

142

stock market firm and, while he made a modest living, he wasn't really happy there. It was difficult for him to take off time for the Jewish holidays. Every year it was the same thing. They wanted him to work and he refused. Harry was aware of the situation and invited Bennie to work for him. Ben was delighted as was Nettie and, of course, Pincas.

****

Time was going so quickly. The High Holy Days were approaching and Golda was busy preparing for them. Adolph and Jean were active and generous members of the 79th Street Orthodox Shul. Adolph remembered how his father would cry and be embarrassed because he couldn't afford to make a donation to his little shul. "Don't cry Poppa. When I grow up, I'll be rich and I'll give money in your name," Adolph had said as he patted his father's back. Now, that is what he did. He would always tell Pincas.

Harry and Hannah also were very good members of the same shul. Harry and Adolph remained close brothers, but Harry was not at all close with Jean. They kept things pleasant, but not much more.

Claire, Al, Nettie, Ben, Henry and Joe, and of course, the two youngest girls, Amy and Millie, were always together with Golda and Pincas for the holidays. Golda did the cooking and baking in advance to allow her to attend the services. She loved to sit in shul and pray.

She was never taught to read when she lived with Toba. She never had any kind of education. When

143

she married Pincas, she would listen to him and she picked up a bit. Later on, as she attended services, she was able to memorize all the prayers. She was just delighted that she was able to participate.

On the High Holy Days, Golda sat in shul for the entire service. Claire and Nettie took care of the meal most of which was already cooked. Only the salad and chopped eggplant had to be prepared. Nettie was the best putlegella (*eggplant*) maker in the family. Amy and Millie set the table and helped wherever they were needed.

On this day, Nettie was busy chopping the onions and roasted eggplant in the large wooden bowl on the backless chair. She added some salad oil and went to the cabinet for a platter leaving the eggplant on the chair.

"Listen! Listen!" The little woman who lived across the street came running into the kitchen. "I have a letter from my father. Listen!" And without looking, she sat down on the chair into the bowl of eggplant.

Emotions were many. Nettie groaned, "My putlegella! What will I do? Everyone expects it."

The two girls were laughing. It was a funny sight. Poor Mrs. Cohen, dripping with salad, was beside herself completely ignoring the letter.

"Oh, help me please. I'm so sorry. I didn't notice anything on the chair."

Nettie scraped what she could off Mrs. Cohen's dress and gave her a damp towel to clean herself, all the while thinking what to do with the eggplant, which had diminished in size.

"Don't worry, Mrs. Cohen. Just go home and change your clothes. It will be O.K." She was trying hard not to show her disappointment.

Pincas, Golda and the boys came home from shul and sat down.

"Nettie, you outdid yourself with this eggplant. It's absolutely delicious," said Henry. The men around the table echoed his remarks.

The women did not touch it. The girls tried to stifle their laughter. "What's so funny?" Al wanted to know. He didn't get an answer then, but some weeks later the putlegella story was told. Everyone had a good laugh.

****

The shul was always full on Simchas Torah. Children marched around holding flags and apples. Men carried the torahs and sang Jewish songs as they walked. There was such a joyous feeling. Everyone was happy. Pincas stood with his sons behind him waiting for their turn to carry a Torah. As he held the scroll, he saw Henry, Joe, Ben, and Al one behind the other all holding a Torah. He hugged and kissed the Torah he was holding in gratitude. "Thank you dear G-d for this blessing."

The girls, Claire, Nettie, Amy, Millie, and Golda were waiting for them to pass by so they could kiss the torah and them. When Pincas came to

Claire, she put her arms around him and whispered in his ear, "Poppa, I'm pregnant".

Pincas raised the Torah high and with tears of happiness exclaimed, "Thank G-d."

The congregants didn't know what was going on, but they were so moved by the emotion, they cried and were saying mazel tov, too. That evening after services there was such gayety, such singing and wine drinking. At last Claire and Al would be blessed with a child.

She gave birth to a beautiful boy and called him Robert Efreham. Nettie's baby was named Robert Lawrence and they became known as Big Bobby and Little Bobby.

Golda was happy in her role of grandma. The children loved her and saw her everyday. Claire and Nettie shopped for her and spent afternoons at the house. When the children were a little older, Golda prepared a small area in the back yard where she dug up the earth so that it was soft. She gave the boys a spoon, an old strainer, and a pot. They had a marvelous time playing in the good earth.

****

"Pina, Pina," called Golda. "I have wonderful news." Pincas was in the bedroom starting to take off his brace. It was early evening and after dinner he couldn't wait to try to make himself a little more comfortable.

"What is it Golda?" he asked. Golda came into the room her eyes bright with excitement.

146

"Harry just called. Hannah went to the doctor today and found out that she's pregnant. Mazel tov."

Pincas was unraveling the bandage from his foot. He stopped and smiled. "Mazel tov. She should have a healthy baby and she should be well."

"You know Pina, when Martin was born she was told not to have any more children. I hope all will go well. Harry is very worried. He's happy but he is scared. He loves his family so much. G-d should help them. Everything should be good."

"Our family is getting bigger thank the good Lord." said Pina. "Our youngest is already fifteen. We have been lucky with our family. Please G-d may it continue."

Nine months went by quickly and Harry called to say that Hannah was in the hospital giving birth. It was in the evening about seven o'clock. The family was home when the call came in and everyone was excited. He sounded nervous and Golda tried to assure him that soon Hannah and the child would be fine. She was worried herself because it was taking so long. Golda sat by the phone praying that the good news would come soon.

The phone rang and she grabbed it. With her heart pounding she said, "Hello Harry?"

There were a few seconds of quiet and then a sobbing. Harry stammered, "Mom, Hannah died. She had a hemorrhage. Momma, she's gone. Oh G-d I can't believe it. Momma, what will I do without her? Oh poor Martin. Oh my G-d." Then he hung up the phone.

Golda was stunned and shocked. She started to cry and call out to the family. "Pina, Henry, Joey oy vey! Gut e nu. Hannah is gone. She died. Amy, Millie, oh poor Harry."

She couldn't control herself. She wept out loud and couldn't be consoled. Pincas hobbled out of the bedroom and went to Golda. He put his arms around her and held her close. Tears were rolling down his face.

"Henry, Joe, please go to the hospital and stay with your brother. Try to bring him here. If you can't, then stay with him."

To his sobbing wife he said as he rocked her in his arms, "Goldala, try to control yourself for the children's sake. Try to be strong. We must accept G-d's will. Her days on earth were ended. Poor, darling, young woman. There's nothing we can do. We must help Harry. Golda, do you know anything about the baby? Did Harry say anything?"

"No Pina, he didn't. And I didn't ask. Oh my poor son. How will he go on without Hannah?"

"Sha, Sha Goldala. G-d will make him strong so he can be a good father."

Henry and Joe came home with Harry who went into his mother's outstretched arms. They cried and held each other.

"Harry, is there a baby?" Pincas asked softly.

"Yes, a little boy. Poor little kid without a mother," he answered with a sob." I don't know how I can go on."

Pincas said, "You will go on Harry. G-d will make you strong. You have two sons and you have to take care of them, provide for them and give them lots of love. Where is Martin? Is he at your home or at your in-laws?"

Harry answered, "At my sister in-law's home. I brought him and his nurse over when I drove Hannah to the hospital. They were going to stay there until Hannah came home."

The Rosenblatts arranged for the funeral and burial on their family plot. The shiva week was at their home. It was a very sad week. The only thing that brought a smile to Harry's face was when Miss Cotch, the nurse, brought Martin to visit. He was a happy little boy and his father adored him.

Martin looked around the room and not seeing Hannah asked, "Mommy?" Everyone in the room had tears in their eyes. Harry picked him up and held him tightly. Then he told Miss Cotch to take him out.

The new baby was still in the hospital. He was a darling little boy. The doctor assured Harry that he would be able to take care of the clubfoot with a cast. In time, he would be just fine. Harry took his son home after the bris. He was named Hanley after his mother. Miss Cotch was an excellent nurse and took good care of both boys.

Hannah's sister, Rose, wanted to adopt the children giving Harry all visiting rights. Harry became furious. "No one can have my children. I love them. I'll take care of them. They'll have everything that they need and more."

He cut off his relationship with the Rosenblatts because of that. He was so frightened that they might try to take his boys from him. He was with them constantly. He was home every evening right after work and on weekends.

He often went for a walks with the two boys and Miss Cotch. Hanley was in the carriage and Martin would sit in a seat attached to the handle bar.

One Sunday, as they were walking on Broadway, they came to the corner of the street and Miss Cotch said, "Mr. Meirowitz would you mind helping me with the carriage? It's too heavy for me."

"Of course," said Harry. But as he did so, he noticed her smile. He also noticed she had put on lipstick. He felt a bit uneasy because she was acting differently, a little coy. He didn't like it.

That evening he called his mother. "Mom I want to talk to Henry. I want him to stay with me from Monday to Friday. Maybe Amy or Millie could come on the weekend."

Golda thought. I can't ask Amy, a nineteen-year-old girl, to go to her brother's house on weekends to protect him from the governess. Amy was already working in the Place for Harry.

I could ask Millie, Oh my, how can I tell this child to spend Friday after school until Sunday evening in New York with her brother? That was the time she had with her sister. On the other hand, how could I let her my down? Harry had had such tragedy. This poor young man is so sad; his two little sons are motherless. The baby had to wear a little brace on his foot because it turned in. Oh please G-d, help me do the right thing. Let it all be fine.

This is so hard, she thought, sighing deeply, but there was no other choice. This has to be done. I'll tell her as soon as she comes home from Claire's store.

"Millie, is that you?" Golda was in the kitchen peeling apples for her famous strudel. "Honey, come in I have to talk to you."

"What's up Mom?" Millie took a slice of apple that was well seasoned with spice and cinnamon. "Ummm-good" she said as she helped herself to another.

Golda took a breath and said, "Millie, your brother Harry is having a problem with Miss Cotch. She seems to be flirting with him and he is very uneasy about it. He called and asked if Henry could stay at his house during the week and if you would stay with him over the weekend." Golda stopped and looked at her daughter.

Millie looked back at her mother and said, "I can't believe what I'm hearing. She's an old woman, that Miss Cotch. What would she want with our Harry?"

Golda smiled at her youngest daughter. "What would she want—only his money and maybe his name. She might have ideas about getting married to him, who knows? In the mean time poor Harry is very upset. He can't let her go because she is wonderful with the boys, and he can't live alone because he is scared. Do you see what a problem he has?"

Millie looked at her mother's beautiful face which was full of concern right now. "Gosh Mom, it must be hard to be a mother. There is so much to worry about. If a woman has a lot of kids like you, golly there sure are a lot of problems."

"Oh, Malkala, it's all very worthwhile. Especially when one is blessed with children like your Poppa and I have. Of course we worry. All parents do. But what about the joys? Believe me there are plenty. Would you be willing to go and help Harry? I know you love the children."

"I sure do love them. We all do. I'll do whatever you or Harry want me to. I just can't understand that woman. I'm really shocked. Well, all I can say is that you are one great mom, and I love you."

"Thank you, momalia. I love you too with all my heart. I want all my children to be well and happy and care for each other."

"Want to help me with this strudel or do you have something to do?"

"I would love to help you, but I'd like to finish my homework so I can be with Amy when she comes home from work." explained Millie as she grabbed a few slices of apple and started to leave. "See you."

Golda was so relieved that Harry's problem was resolved. She attacked her dough with renewed vigor. Oh, thank G-d, she thought. Millie is such a dear girl, with a good heart. Who knows how long she'll be needed there. Maybe Harry will meet a young woman, fall in love again, and provide his little boys with a mother. Harry is young, handsome, and very comfortable. He is a very good catch for a woman. Golda was just finishing her baking when Pincas entered.

"Golda, could we have cup of demitasse? I would like to talk a little."

"Sure Pina, just let me put this strudel in the oven." Golda put the pan in the oven and took out her little pot for the demitasse. She used a strong coffee and added stcoria (*chicory*). It took just a few minutes to make, then she strained it. Golda served it in beautiful demitasse cups they had brought from Europe. They were made of fine china with raised designs of flowers, stars etc. in gold and vivid colored paint.

"Delicious," exclaimed Pincas, as he took a sip and placed the cup on its beautiful little saucer. "You know Golda, people have approached me asking if Harry would be willing to meet a young woman. I didn't know what to say."

"I was just thinking about the very same thing. I think it's too soon. I imagine he would become angry. Let's leave him alone for a while. Millie is going to be with him over the weekends. Let's wait. He's renting a house in Long Beach for the summer. The children will love it. Jean and Adolph also rented a house there, and Nettie took a little apartment at the beach. I hope to G-d they get along well."

"Every thing will be all right, don't worry," said Pincas. "Getting back to Harry, a man should have a wife. He is young and needs to have a full life."

"All in time Pina, all in time." Golda answered. "Millie will spend the summer at the beach. It will be nice for her and it will be good for Harry. Maybe he'll start going out a little. He sure has a lot to offer a woman."

Pincas sighed. "Whatever you said is true. But Golda he has to have mazel to meet the right person. I pray he should."

They finished their coffee and as Golda started to clear the table the phone rang. It was Nettie.

"Mom, it's so beautiful here. You and Poppa must come. You can stay at Harry's or at my apartment. It doesn't matter, just come. The children are so happy". Golda was glad to hear from her daughter and very pleased that all was so good.

"Oh darling, I'm so happy that you and the children are enjoying the beach. Yes, dear Poppa and I will come out for a weekend. Henry will drive us. I'll let you know when. Thanks for calling, my love to all." She hung up the phone.

"Thank G -d it seems to be working out well with the children."

"I told you not to worry." smiled Pincas.

The plan was that Henry would drive Golda and Pincas to Long Beach. He would stay for a few hours and then drive home leaving the folks and returning for them on the following Sunday. Golda packed a valise of clothing for herself and for Pincas as well as medications that he might need. She also packed a large box of goodies for all the children.

Henry drove to his brother Harry's first. He visited and played a bit with Martin and Hanley. Then he left for a visit to Nettie and Benny's.

Golda and Pincas were just delighted to see the two little boys. Martin and Hanley were beautiful children and seemed quite happy. Millie was enjoying being there, too.

"Tell Nettie we'll see her soon," called Golda to Henry as he pulled away.

When Henry came to the four-family apartment house, he saw Nettie, Benny, and the two children standing outside.

"Hi Hennie, it's so great to see you. Are Momma and Poppa here too?" asked Nettie.

"Yes," Henry answered. "They're at Harry's. You'll see them soon. You all look so good and the kids are so nice and tan."

Just then a beautiful girl came out of the building. "Hi Nettie," she said, as she gently patted the head of Nettie's little daughter Rona. "How are you?" she asked.

All the while, Henry was staring at this girl. He couldn't take his eyes off her.

"Who is she, Nettie?" he asked.

"Jane this is my brother Henry. Hennie, meet our neighbor, Jane."

"Hello Jane," said Henry making a gesture of a bow. "It's a real pleasure to meet you."

"Same here," replied Jane with a big smile on her face.

"Want to go for a walk on the beach?" asked Henry.

"I would love to," she quickly answered.

Nettie smiled as they walked away. "He really fell for her, not that I blame him. She's a beauty don't you think so, Ben?"

Henry spent the whole day with Jane. He asked her out to dinner and decided not to go home that night. "Nettie, is it OK if I stay over at your place tonight? Jane and I would like to go out this evening."

"Of course. You are most welcome," Nettie assured him.

Henry brought Jane to his brother's home and introduced Jane to his mother and father. They could feel Henry's excitement over this girl and Golda was glad for him. She spoke to Jane about her family and her ambitions. She could tell that Jane was feeling a bit nervous because she was clasping her hands and releasing them as she answered, always looking at Henry who had moved to the back of the room to speak to Harry.

"You know, Mrs. Meirowitz , I'm going out with Henry tonight. Do you think my hair looks all right? I want to look good. I'm so excited." She was talking quickly and seemed nervous. "I really should do my hair myself. I always do. My Mom doesn't like me to spend money on beauty parlors. I don't know what to do."

Golda looked at this beautiful girl and smiled. "My dear, what could a beauty shop do to make you look better? Your hair is shiny and you have it styled very well. But I understand how you feel. You look lovely to me, but why not have it done? It will make you feel glamorous."

Golda laughed and patted Jane's shoulder lovingly. "If it's a question of money, please let me. It's my pleasure."

Golda reached into her purse, pulled out some bills and put them into Jane's hand. "No need to mention it to Henry. Just do it. It will be our secret," Golda whispered.

"Oh thank you so much, you are the greatest," Jane whispered back as she gave Golda a kiss. "Henry," she called, "we have to go if you want me to be ready tonight."

Henry quickly said goodbye to his family and waited for Jane to come. She whispered another thank you to Golda and left with Henry.

"What a doll your mother is," Jane said as soon as they were seated in the car.

I'm glad you feel that way because you are going to see a lot of her," answered Henry happily.

They saw a great deal of each other. Golda and Pincas weren't a bit surprised when Henry told them that he was in love with Jane and wanted to put a ring on her finger. He told them that her parents, Mr. and Mrs. Zahn were fine people. They had another daughter and a son younger than Jane. Mr. Zahn worked for a milk company and earned a modest living.

Golda and Pincas were happy for Henry and even though he had many opportunities to marry rich girls, they liked Jane. Both felt it was more important to be in love than to have a lot of money.

They met the Zahns and found them to be lovely people. The wedding date was set for December and the family was very excited. Golda invited the Zahns to the house for a dinner so all the children could meet each other.

When Jean heard that Mr. Zahn worked for Sheffield Farms, she began to refer to Jane as the milkman's daughter. Golda didn't like it, but there was nothing she could do.

****

The summer was almost over. Harry would go out on a date occasionally. He had met a lovely woman who was a widow without children. She was blond, soft spoken and seemed to care for

Harry and the boys a great deal. Harry really liked her and told his parents all about Florrie and his intentions of marrying her.

Golda and Pincas were very happy for Harry. "That's wonderful news Harry. Mazel tov." Golda said. "I wish you lots of luck. We would love to meet this young lady. Invite her for dinner.

Pincas was equally pleased, but a little concerned. He put his arm around him and said, "Harry, she is a widow without children and therefore, must have the ceremony of Halitza performed by her brother-in-law.

"Poppa, what's this about?" asked Harry. I'll tell you my son," answered Pincas. "Halitza is a ritual in the bible which requires that when a man who is married dies childless, his brother must marry his widow in order to build his brother's house. If the brother-in-law is already married, or willfully refuses to marry the widow, then the ceremony of Halitza is performed. You see, Harry, the idea is for the brother-in-law to have a child with the widow and in that way her late husband's line is preserved."

"Tell me Poppa, what do we have to do? Just tell me. Florrie will do anything I ask her to do."

"Harry, that's fine, but it is not that simple. First of all, the brother-in-law has to be willing, and he may want to be compensated. If that is the case, there will be money involved. Will she be able to give him what he might ask for? Will you? I must say when we came to America, you know we came because your Uncle Meyer died and Aunt Rose asked me to perform the ceremony of

Halitza, it never occurred to me to ask for money. I wouldn't think of it. However, some men do, and some are very greedy. There has been many a widow who never could marry because of that."

"My, my! Dus raidala draught stzch (*history repeats itself*)," Golda remarked. "Pina, do you remember when Rose's letter came and you thought you would go to America, give Halitza and then come back to Romania?"

"I do remember Golda. You said if I go, we all go," smiled Pincas. "I'm glad you insisted."

"Wow," exclaimed Harry. "It sounds pretty heavy. Hope we can work it out. We do care for each other, and I think it will be good for the boys. Poppa, you'll tell us what we and her brother-in-law have to do."

"I will Harry; I will tell you right now." Pina took a deep breath and began. "The ceremony included three people-the widow, the brother-in-law, and the rabbi. The brother-in-law is asked if he will marry the widow. His answer depends on his status. If he is already married, he can't. If he is not willing, he must perform the ceremony of Halitza which then permits her to marry whomever she pleases.

The widow takes of the brother-in-law's shoe, throws it down, and spits on it. This is a form of degradation since he has refused to perform his duty. This is what has to be done, Harry."

"I can't understand it, but if that's what has to be done, we'll do it," he answered.

Harry went home and promptly told Florrie about the ritual of Halitza and what she would have to do. Florrie was very excited and assured Harry that she would take of it.

When she approached her brother-in-law she was dismayed at his reaction. "I'll think about it," Sam said. "What is his name again and where is his business located?"

Florrie remembered what Harry's father had said about some men demanding money and she became nervous.

"Why do you want to know about his business?" she asked.

"You don't think I'm going to do this stuff for nothing," he retorted. "I think it is crazy myself, but I might do it if I compensated. I'll let you know."

Florrie became upset. "Please Sam, don't make any trouble. I love him and his two little boys and I want to marry him. Tell me what you want and I'll give it to you."

Sam laughed, "You don't have enough money to pay me. As I said, I'll let you know."

"Oh Harry," Florrie wailed as she told him what Sam had said. "I can't imagine what he is going to ask for. I offered to pay him, but he refused."

"Don't worry, Florrie. I'll take care of it. I'll pay him what he wants and then we'll get married," Harry said as he kissed her cheek.

She threw her arms around him and exclaimed, "Oh, I do love you so much."

Pincas was right. It wasn't that simple. Sam found out that Harry Meirowitz was a rich man and decided to get as much money as he possibly could from him. When Harry called him he told Harry that he would give Halitza for five thousand dollars. Harry was appalled.

"How can you ask for so much money? That's extortion," Harry exclaimed

Sam was enjoying this power he suddenly felt. Sam answered him firmly, "You can pay it. I looked you up in Dunn and Bradstreet. You are a rich man."

Harry was becoming very angry, but was trying to control himself. "I'll give you half and let's get it over with," he said.

"Nothing doing," said Sam. "five grand or nothing."

"I won't do it," Harry replied.

"Why can't we get married without Halitza?" Florrie wanted to know.

"We can't. My father says it is not allowed. It says so in the bible," Harry answered sadly. "Maybe it will still work out."

It didn't. They stopped seeing each other and that was the end of a beautiful life they could have had together.

****

Once again friends and matchmakers called Pincas with eligible women. Harry once again, rented a house for the summer in Long Beach. Adolph and Jean did the same. It was so beautiful there. One morning Jean called Harry's house and invited Millie to have breakfast with her. Millie thanked her for the invitation, but explained that she had already eaten with the boys.

"Come over anyway, Millie," she said. "You can leave the kids with the housekeeper for a little while."

Millie agreed to go and made sure that it was alright with Annie, the housekeeper. Annie was a good, kind person and really loved the boys. "Go," she said. "Martin and Hanley will be fine. Don't worry."

It was a beautiful morning and Millie started out in a happy mood, waving and throwing kisses to the boys. It was a short walk to Jean's house and when Millie arrived, Jean was at her dining room table eating her breakfast. It was a large bowl of corn flakes topped with strawberries and bananas.

"Good morning Millie, how are you?" she asked.

"Fine thank you, and you?" Millie asked. "Where is Connie?"

"She's out with her governess. Tell me how is your brother? Bumming around with girls?" She was stuffing her mouth with the cereal and grinned as she asked.

Millie stood up and said loudly, "Don't you call my brother a bum. He's a fine man, and a wonderful father. I'm going home!"

"Oh calm down. Sit here and just let me finish my breakfast. Then we'll go to the store. I want to buy you a pair of shoes. You'd like that wouldn't you? And please, don't say anything about what I said. I was joking," Jean said.

"I don't want shoes and definitely not from you. You don't have to bribe me. I would be ashamed to repeat what you said. I'm leaving," Millie retorted as she headed for the door.

"Please, stay a little longer and don't be so angry. It's wonderful the way you protect your brother," Jean said.

Millie stopped, turned, and faced her sister-in-law. Mom would be upset if she heard me speak like that to Jean, she thought to herself.

"I'm sorry I acted so fresh, Jean, but I can't stand to have anyone in my family criticized especially when it's not true. And I really do have to leave. I promised to play ball with Martin when I got home. I'm not angry. Bye Jean."

Millie left and walked home quickly. She was greeted with hugs from the boys and she warmly responded. She loved those two little boys and they regarded her as a big sister.

****

As summer was coming to an end, Henry and Jane were busy planning their wedding. Henry was not living with Harry any longer since Miss Cotch had given up trying to win Harry's adoration and quit her job. Although there had been a few nurses after her, no one made the children as happy as Millie. At this time, he had only the housekeeper and Millie to care for the children and the household.

Millie loved her brother, but she feared him at the same time. He had a temper and he lost it at times. He was a perfectionist and ran his home like his business.

"Where is the milk bill?" he would demand loudly. Millie would literally tremble as she produced it. Harry was often referred to as a diamond in the rough. He was very good to his sister and was grateful for her help with his little pups (his name the boys).

Millie decided to leave school and stay at Harry's to care for the boys. This pleased Harry and delighted Martin and Hanley. She later regretted not continuing with her education, but at the time, this decision seemed right. She had become so emotionally involved with Harry's plight and was so attached to Martin and Hanley, that she felt she had no other alternative. No one in the family objected or even encouraged her to finish high school.

Golda came to New York once a week to spend the day with Millie and the children. She would go to the park with them and stay for the evening. Harry and Pincas would come from work and they would have dinner together. Sometimes Joe, Nettie and Ben, or Amy would come later and visit. They would have coffee and then take Golda and Pincas home. It would be a very pleasant day for Millie and the children.

****

Henry and Jane had a beautiful wedding and settled in Flatbush. Jane busied herself visiting her parents, her in-laws and friends. About a year passed and she gave birth to a beautiful little girl, whom they named Sharon. Life was good for them.

****

At home, over their demitasse, Golda and Pincas discussed their children. "Pina, I think Joey has a girlfriend. Remember, I told you about her? She has no father, but her mother is very religious. She seems to be a very nice girl. I think he is in love."

That very evening Pincas was in his room starting to prepare for bed. He called to Joe, "Come in here. I want to talk to you."

"Coming Poppa," answered Joe. He was in the kitchen and quickly ran up the steps to his father's bedroom. "What's up Pop?" he asked.

Pincas was sitting in his chair bandaging his foot. He stopped and looked at his handsome son proudly and said, "Joe, Momma told me have been seeing a girl for quite a while. She also told me that she has no father, but has four sisters, a brother, and a very religious mother. Is that right?"

Joe smiled. "Right, Poppa. She is a great girl and we love each other," he said.

"Well, why not ask her to the house so we can all meet her?" asked Pincas. "Now that Henry is married, you are next in line." Pincas saw the look of happiness come over his son's face.

"I'd love to do that and I will," Joe happily answered. "Ethel will be very happy to come and meet the family. Thanks, Pop."

With that, he bounded out of the room. It was too late to go to Ethel's house and tell her the good news. He would see her in the morning. He was so excited he couldn't fall asleep.

Ethel was happy when Joe told her the news, but she was nervous about meeting his parents. She knew his sisters, but his mother and father scared her.

"Don't worry, Ethel," Joe said, "they will love you."

When he brought her home for Friday night dinner, everything was lovely, happy and comfortable. Pincas was interested in her mother. He asked where she came from. He was a bit disappointed when he learned they were Glitzianas, but he tried to hide it. "We would love to meet your family," he said.

They did meet shortly after and found they really liked each other. Golda and Pina found Mrs. Rosenrich to be a fine, intelligent Orthodox woman and they all bonded. They planned a wedding date. Everyone was delighted, especially Joe and Ethel.

"Ethel," said her mother, "you will go to the Mickvah (*ritual bath*) just before the wedding."

"What's that?" Ethel asked.

"Every Jewish girl goes to the Mikvah before her marriage," her mother explained. "It is a tradition and a religious requirement. Years ago there were no facilities for bathing. At the Mikvah nails and hair are cut for cleanliness. Seeing her daughter's eyes open wide in astonishment she quickly added, "Oh they won't do that to you now, but maybe just your toenails. You will go into a pool and a prayer is said. Its not painful. Its a beautiful ritual."

"Ugh," Ethel groaned. "I'm not going. Joe wouldn't want me to go,"

"Oh yes you will," her mother said calmly.

When Ethel discussed this with Joe he emphatically stated, "You will not go!"

Ethel had a friend who owned a beauty shop and offered to do her hair the evening before the wedding. It was Saturday night, before her wedding, and Ethel was sitting under the dryer when her mother walked into the beauty parlor. She walked over to the dryer and knocked on the hood. Ethel pushed up the hood and saw it was her mother.

"Ethel," said her mother, "come, we are going to the Mikvah."

In a high pitched hysterical tone Ethel cried out, "I am not going. I told you I wouldn't go. And Joe doesn't want me to go either!" With that she pulled the dryer hood back down again.

Mrs. Rosenrich stood quietly next to the dryer and again knocked on the hood. Ethel pushed up the hood again and this time was crying. "Leave me alone. I am not going."

Her mother calmly said, "We are going. And if you don't go, I will not be at your wedding."

Very tearfully Ethel came out from under the dryer and said to her friend Yetta, "I guess I have to go. Oh, I hate this." Yetta assured her she would fix her hair in the morning.

When Joe heard about this he was furious. He waited for her to come home. He was practically in tears himself. He said, "Ethel, take a good shower. You poor kid." He was so angry at her mother he couldn't even speak to her. He just left.

****

Pincas was in his room binding his foot with a bandage and thinking about his life. We are so fortunate Golda and I. Our children are respectable, well behaved, and responsible. Thank the good Lord. We only have the two girls Amy and Millie left at home. I hope they stay around a while, but if they find their ba shertas (*soul mates*) then that will be alright, too.

Harry and the rest of the children wanted their parents to go Saratoga Springs on a vacation. Pincas always refused.

"What do I need a vacation for?" asked Pincas." I have everything I need right here."

"Poppa," Harry would say. "It would be so good for Momma. She could use a change. She would rest and enjoy meeting people. It would be good for you." But Pincas would not consent to go.

Finally, he decided to try it. He had spoken to someone in the Place and they told him that the water was marvelous and so good for the stomach. They enjoyed the week so much that they made a reservation for the following year.

Amy was working for Harry and her vacation was coming up. "Micky," Amy said. "How would you like to go with me on my vacation? It will be your sweet sixteen birthday present from me. We'll go to White Row Lake House. You will love it. I told Mom about this and she said it was fine for you to go."

"Oh thank you, Amy! I'm so excited. What do I wear? I never was away to a hotel. Gosh Amy, I'm scared. I have to make sure Harry will be able to manage with the boys."

Millie was talking fast and Amy started to laugh. "Calm down, Micky. Everything will be fine. Harry already knows. He is glad that you are going. The kids will miss you and you'll miss them, but we need a little vacation together, too."

Amy gave her little sister a big hug. "I'm so excited. Everything is going to be great. As for the clothes, we'll shop! Don't worry. I'll take care of everything. This'll be fun." She smiled a big happy smile.

Millie was so happy she jumped up and down. "Oh," she said. "I'm the one who is really excited. I never dreamed that I would go to the mountains with you. Oh Amy, you are the best sister and best friend I ever had." She looked at Amy lovingly.

"Me too," answered Amy smiling again. "Now you have to listen to me and do what I say. When we get there, the guys may ask you what room we are in. Do not tell them, understand? That's very important."

"Why not?" Millie wanted to know.

"Just don't tell. That's all. Don't worry about it Micky. Everything will be fine."

"OK, I won't say anything," but she looked puzzled.

The day finally came and with much excitement they left for the train. When they came to Elenville, a bus was waiting for them. There were quite a number of young people getting on. The boys all eyed Amy and gave her a warm hello as the bus started off to White Row Lake House.

No sooner did Amy register and get the room number, when a young man came over to Millie and asked, "Hey Red, what room are you in?"

Forgetting completely what her sister had told her, she said clearly "room 321."

This was immediately followed by a hard shove from Amy. "Come on Mickey," she whispered, "now we'll have to push the dresser against the door."

"Why?" asked Millie, "I still don't understand."

"Never mind. Come on."

Millie followed her sister to room 321. It was a nice room with two beds, a chair, and a dresser. They had their own very nice and bathroom. Millie thought it was wonderful.

"What do we do now, Amy?" she asked.

"We unpack, and then we'll go down to the lobby and socialize."

"Amy, I'm sorry I goofed with the room. I forgot what you told me. Please don't be angry with me," she pleaded. She looked so worried and sad. "Bet you're sorry you took me along."

Amy put her arm around her sister and said gently, "I'm not angry Micky, and I'm not sorry. Let's go."

When they got to the lobby, many of the guests were assembled on the porch. It was a lovely evening, cool with a smell of jasmine that filling the air. Millie was so happy. She was wearing make up and had her hair in an upsweep. She looked much older than sixteen.

"Hey Red," called a young man, "introduce me to your kid sister."

This made Millie feel proud and she responded with, "Sure, if she wants me to."

Amy was already talking to some boys and seemed very much at ease. Oh, Millie thought, how beautiful she is and so poised. I love her.

They went into the dinning room for dinner, and it was delicious. As they were finishing dessert, a young man came to the table. He asked Millie if she would come out with him when she finished her dinner. Millie was so surprised that for a moment she couldn't respond. She looked at her sister and receiving a nod she said, "O.K."

As they went out to the porch, Millie was very quiet and a bit nervous. She tried to act relaxed, but it was hard. This young man however, was tall and handsome and very calm and sure of himself. "My name is Bob. Bob Young. What's yours?" he asked her with a smile on his face.

"Millie Meirowitz," she answered softly. Wow, she thought, he's good looking, and he must be old, at least in his twenties. Aloud she asked, "Where do you live?"

"In Flatbush," he answered, "and you?

"I live in Borough Park .We are practically neighbors," she answered.

Finally she started to relax and enjoy being on the porch, watching the people coming out of the dining room. Bob invited her to join him in the casino where they had a band, drinks, and then a show. Millie was excited and wanted to go but also needed to see Amy.

"I'll go in just a second, but first I want to see my sister. Oh there she is. I'll be right back."

She went over to Amy. "Hi Amy. That guy asked me to go to the casino with him. Is that all right? And what are you going to do?"

"Of course it's alright Micky. Go. Have a good time. Don't worry about me. I'm going to be with Sid. You know him. I'll be in the casino, too. See you later, Mick."

It was a real treat for Millie. She had never been in a place like this. A band was playing familiar music, people were dancing, and some were just talking in groups. It was so friendly and happy.

"Oh I just love being here," she said.

Bob smiled at her delight and said "I'm glad you like it so much." He thought she was cute, good looking, and he couldn't tell, but he surmised she was fun to be with. "Would you like to dance?" he asked.

"Oh yes, "she answered. "I love to dance." She was a good dancer, thanks to her brother Henry. He taught her and danced with her at home a lot.

"You dance very well, so light on your feet, and so easy to lead," Bob said as he twirled her around. She followed him very easily.

"Thank you," she answered happily.

They finished the set, and Bob led her out to take in the cool breeze and peacefulness of the evening. He took a deep breath. "Lovely out here isn't it?" he asked as he put his arm around her.

She became nervous and whispered, "Yes it is. I wonder where Amy is. Maybe I should go in and look for her," she said quickly.

"Wait a bit. Let's talk for a minute," he said as he dropped his arm. "Do you like horses? I ride and I would love to take you horse back riding tomorrow. Do you ride?"

Millie was grateful that he had removed his arm. "No, but I was on a pony for a picture once."

He smiled. "I love to ride. These last two days I rode a great horse and I want to ride him again tomorrow. Will you come with me?" he asked.

Millie answered, "OK, if you want me to. I might spoil your ride."

"Don't worry, you won't. It'll be fun. I'll meet you on the porch at eight. OK?" he asked.

"Oh yes, thank you." She was excited and her voice showed it. They walked back to the main building where Bob gave her a quick kiss on her cheek and said good night. Millie stood still for a few minutes and smiling she went to the room to wait for Amy.

The next morning Millie and Bob set out for the stables. "I hope they don't give me a wild horse," she stated nervously. "After all, I never really went horse back riding."

"Oh, I'll take care of that," he laughed. When they came to the stables, Bob spoke to the attendant. A black horse was brought out for Millie and Bob helped her on. Bob was given the same horse that he had ridden before and he was very happy.

"All set? Let's go." He started to move out slowly, but Millie's horse didn't budge. "Gidyup," she commanded. But he didn't move. The stable man gave the horse a kick and the horse went into a trot. "Oh, oh, I'm going to fall off," Millie called out. "I'm going to fall."

"You won't fall off," laughed Bob "just hold on to the reins and relax."

Millie did what he told her to do and she found herself enjoying the ride. "I' m going to take a fast ride be back in a few minutes, OK?"

"Sure," she said, but she didn't mean it. She was very nervous and didn't trust the horse.

Bob galloped off and she just sat on Blackie holding on to the reins. When she saw him in the distance, she was very impressed with how well he rode, how handsome he looked on the horse, and how nice he was.

Bob returned and approached her with a smile. "Did you ride?" he asked.

Millie smiled back and answered shyly, "To tell the truth, I mostly sat right here on Blackie, but I did enjoy it a lot. Thank you for inviting me."

"You're a cute girl. Too bad I'm leaving this afternoon. We could have done this again," he said. Millie didn't say anything but she was hoping that he would ask for her phone number or say something about seeing her some other time. They returned the horses and walked back to the hotel.

"Well, I've got to pack, have lunch and then I'm off," he said. "It sure was a pleasure to meet you. Hope we meet again somewhere." And giving her a quick kiss on the cheek, he turned and went into the hotel.

Millie stood still and her eyes filled with tears. I guess he didn't like me. Why should he? I'm dumb. I don't know much of anything and I'm not pretty or anything. She was berating herself when Bob came out.

"Millie, I'm sorry I was so abrupt. I just realized I never told you anything about myself. You see, I came here for a complete rest. I was on the verge of a nervous breakdown. I'm engaged to a wonderful girl. I hope to be married in about six months and it really was nice to be in your company," he said. "You are a very lovely girl and some day a lucky guy is going to come your way. I'm sorry I didn't tell you all that before. Please forgive me."

Millie put out her hand. "I'm so glad you told me. I wish you good luck and lots of happiness." She felt better now and was happy for him. He sure was a nice guy. That girl is real lucky to get him she thought.

She was standing on the porch and looked around her. This is a beautiful place. The air was clean and the grass so green and sweet smelling.

She had never been a guest in a hotel before. She walked around the grounds to the lake. It was large and peaceful. Water lilies were bobbing up and down in the water. So many young boys and girls were in rowboats on the lake. Oh, she thought, I wish Momma could see this place. She would love it.

Millie saw Amy on the lake with Sid. Amy looked happy and Millie was glad. They had two more days of this paradise and then home.

The hotel had a ping-pong table and Millie was a very good player. She had been hoping to get in a good game. As she approached the table, a young man challenged her to a game. Millie won the set. Pleased, she went to her room to shower and get ready for lunch.

The next day was filled with activity and before Amy and Millie realized it, was time to pack.

"Mickey, would you mind if I went out on the lake with Sid before we have lunch and leave?"

"Of course not, Amy. Have a good time," Millie quickly answered. "I'll sit on the porch and read. I love to do that."

As she settled herself on the porch, she noticed some young men getting ready to leave. One of them came over to her and asked, "Where is your sister? I've been looking all over. I want to say good-by."

Millie knew that Amy was on the lake with Sid, so she said, "I'll tell her you had to leave. Do you have her phone number? When he said he did,

Millie said, "Call her when you get home and have a nice ride."

"Don't forget to tell her George was looking for her, and that he'll call her at home, OK?" He seemed so anxious.

"OK, OK," Millie promised. She wished they would leave. One of the boys was bidding farewell to a girl and they were kissing ardently more than once. Finally they pulled away and were gone. The girl stepped back and stood near Millie and wistfully turned to her and asked, "Isn't he wonderful?"

Millie hadn't paid much attention to the fellow, but she answered, "Oh yes, very nice."

Finally, it was time to pack and leave. Many hugs and kisses and vows to keep in touch were exchanged. The bus and train rides went quickly and soon they were home telling Golda about their vacation and the good time they had.

"Who is this George Schwartz? The telephone is exploding. He sounds very nice, but I wish he would stop calling. He must have called six or seven times in the last two hours."

Amy smiled. "We had a wonderful time Mom, and he told me he would call me."

Millie chimed in, "He was looking for her before he left and kept asking me where she was. I knew she was on the lake with some guy, but I wouldn't tell him. He's very nice though."

Amy was laughing and she said, "If he calls again, I'll go out with him so you'll meet him. Let's unpack Micky. It's getting late." She started to go upstairs. She wasn't at the top of the steps when the phone rang.

"That must be him again, Amy. Do you want to answer it?"

"No Mom, please will you?" answered Amy.

"Hello?" inquired Golda.

"Hello Mrs. Meirowitz. Did Amy come home?"

"Yes, my daughters are home. I'll call Amy to the phone. Just a minute."

They spoke for a while. Amy laughed quite a bit during the phone call. Finally, Amy called out to her mother, "Mom, he's asking for Mickey to go out with us and his friend. OK? Can I ask her? She'll be fine. I'll make sure of that, OK?"

Golda was smiling "If you think it's alright, and she wants to go it's OK with me."

Amy called to her sister, "'Mickey, come here a minute. I want to ask you something."

Millie approached her sister. "What's up Amy?" she asked.

"George invited me out for Labor Day and he asked if you would go too, with one of his friends. Would you like to? Mom said you could. They want to go to Jones Beach to see the show on the bay, *Naughty Marietta*, O.K.?"

"No way, not me. All those boys are short," answered Millie.

Amy returned to the phone and after a few seconds came back to her sister. "The guy George has in mind is the tall one. Come on Mickey, we'll be together. It'll be fun."

Millie always loved to be with her sister and this did sound exciting so she said yes.

Golda was listening to the girls talking and planning and she smiled. How close they were. Amy was so good to her little sister and they loved and respected each other. Golda was sure that Amy would take care of Millie when they went to Jones Beach.

She sighed, wishing Claire and Nettie got along as well. There was a feeling of competition between them, especially with their daughters. They were always comparing, always competing. I don't understand. They both have wonderful children and good husbands. Both live nicely. I wish they were closer.

Golda went to her bedroom and slowly started to undress. Pincas was in bed and Golda thought he was sleeping. "Golda what's wrong? I can tell something is bothering you."

Golda smiled. "Pina, you know me so well. Yes I am a little worried about Claire and Nettie. I think they are jealous about their girls. I don't know why. Rona and Elaine are both so darling, both so bright. Why can't they just enjoy their little girls and see the goodness and dearness of each other's daughter?"

"Golda, come to bed. Everything will work out. You'll see."

Golda and Pina always remained awake until their children returned home. This Sunday evening they were in their beds when they heard the door open and softly close.

"Amy? Millie?" called Golda. "Is that you?"

Millie came bounding into the room. She threw herself on her mother's bosom and sobbed, "Mom, Mom, what do I look like? Some cheap thing? Oh Mom, it was terrible. He kissed me in the dark. We were telling ghost stories, and he grabbed me and kissed me. I couldn't say anything because I was so ashamed. Oh Momma, I feel so awful."

Golda held her daughter tightly in her arms and then as she stroked her gently she said, "Mommila you are so beautiful he couldn't help it. Don't feel so bad. You do not look cheap and you are not cheap. You are a lovely beautiful girl. Now go to sleep dear and have pleasant dreams."

"You think so, Mom?"

"Of course dear," Golda replied.

As Millie was leaving the room feeling so much better, Pina turned to his wife, "Golda, Golda, where did you learn to speak to a child like that? You are so brilliant, so kind. I am so proud of you."

"Pina, what could I say to that poor child at such a late hour? I really don't like it and I'll talk about it to her in the morning. But at this time, I had to let her have a night's sleep."

Pincas smiled. "I guess that's why I love you so much. You always say the right thing."

Golda smiled said, "I love you too, Pina. Good night."

****

George called Amy the next evening and asked her out. In fact he called her every evening. He was falling in love with her and she with him. Amy was happy.

"He's very nice Micky," she said. "We have such a great time when we are together."

The boy that was Millie's date called and when he asked her out she asked him to please hold on a minute. "Mom, that guy, Louis Fain, is on the phone. He asked me out. I'd like to. Should I? Is it OK?"

Golda smiled. A few nights ago this girl was crying and feeling so miserable because this young man kissed her. Now, she wants to go out with him, "Well, Millie dear," she said "it's alright if you want to see him, but don't let him kiss you so much."

"Thanks Mom." Millie ran back to the phone and told Lou she would like to go out with him, but she'd be in New York with her brother's children. She briefly explained Harry's situation. When Lou said that he would come to New York, she accepted the date happily.

Nu, my girls are grown up, Golda thought. Thank G-d. Such good girls. Before we know it Pina and I will be alone in this big house. She looked around and sighed. We had some wonderful years in this house. Raising eight children has been quite a job, but I have enjoyed it. And thank the Lord; they have grown into fine respectable young men and women. We are lucky, Pina and I, especially me. When I think back to Romania and Toba, I shudder at the life I had in her home.

Golda began to reflect back on those early days of her life. She thought to herself, I remember my mother and father and the happy home we had. My brother was so much older than I, and when he married Toba, she had been pleasant and seemed to like me. Oh, did she change. When Father died suddenly, it was very hard for Mother to manage the business. It had been a very good business and we were comfortable. Even though she had help, it was still too difficult for her.

When she became ill and died, oy vey, did my world crumble. My brother was so afraid of Toba, and didn't interfere with anything that went on. My parents' money, used for their children, not me. If it weren't for Pincas, who knows what would have happened to me. She heaved a sigh of both relief and sadness.

****

George became a frequent visitor at the house. Amy liked him, and Millie was happy for her. "Amy," she asked. "Does George say anything? I mean anything serious?"

Amy smiled. "Yes he does, but I want to be sure. He's a great guy and I really like him a lot. We'll see." She hugged her sister and said again "We'll see."

George asked Amy to marry him and Amy accepted. Golda and Pincas were satisfied. They had met the Schwartz family including Edna, George's sister and her husband Oscar and found them to be very fine people. The Schwartz family felt the same way about Golda and Pincas, and they loved Amy.

Plans were made for the wedding. Pincas reserved The Broadway Central Hotel. It was a happy affair. Solomon danced with his beautiful granddaughter, Amy. She was truly a most gorgeous bride. They did a handkerchief dance. Each held a corner of the handkerchief. Millie was the Maid of Honor and Louis was the Best Man.

Amy and George decided to accept Golda and Pincas' invitation to live with them until they could get on their feet. It was good for Golda who was getting a bit tired. Amy was a great help keeping the house clean and being company to her parents. George was a wonderful son-in-law. He drove Pincas wherever he had to go.

One day George was driving Pincas to the doctor and he was pulled over by a police officer for speeding. Please, officer, don't give him a ticket. He is such a good boy. He takes me all over. He's taking me to the doctor," pleaded Pincas.

"Pop, cut it out," begged George as he handed the officer his license.

Pincas continued, "He's my son–in–law. He is so nice to my wife and me. Please let him off."

The officer looked at George who seemed so uncomfortable and said, "O.K. buddy get going. You have enough trouble." Needless to say this story was told many times.

****

Millie and Lou saw each other on the weekends. Lou came to Harry's apartment on Central Park West most of the time. Harry liked him and so did the boys.

On Sundays, the Fain family came together at their Mom and Dad's. Fannie Fain and her husband Elias had five sons. Murray and Meyer were married and had children. Sidney was the youngest and lived with his parents. Ben lived with them since his divorce.

Lou's brother, Murray, didn't have a car, so Lou would drive him, his wife and their little daughter to their home.

One Sunday, Millie and Lou were on the way to pick up Murray and his family when Lou said, "Come up and you'll meet some of my family."

"Now? I'm not dressed," she groaned.

"Don't worry it will be just fine. I'll call and tell them we're coming up. Don't worry you look fine," Lou assured her.

After calling at a pay phone, he came back to the car and said, "They are anxious to meet you, come on."

Millie was very nervous and when she entered the apartment. Lou's mother greeted her with, "Sit down. We'll have tea."

Mille looked for a place to sit. There was only one chair in the kitchen that was unoccupied, but a large pile of newspapers was resting on it. She sat down on the chair. She felt awkward with her feet dangling above the floor.

The sisters-in-law were very friendly and tried to make her feel comfortable, but Mrs. Fain just kept busy. Finally, it was time to leave and take Murray, Sylvia, and little Eleanor home. Millie was glad. They had said good-by and were in the foyer about to go when a man came out of the bedroom.

"Oh, here's my Dad. Pop this is Millie, my friend. Millie, meet my father."

Millie shyly put out her hand. "How do you do?" she said.

"Well, how do you do? If I knew there was such a pretty young lady out here I would have come out sooner," he said, holding and patting her hand. They all said good bye and left.

In the car Sylvia kept light conversation going, talking to Eleanor and Murray, trying to involve Millie and Louie who were quiet. When they got to their apartment, they invited Millie and Lou to come up, but they declined saying they had plans.

As they started to drive away, Lou asked Millie, "What's the matter? You are so quiet."

"Your mother hated me and I looked awful. This was such a mistake for me to come with you." Millie said quietly. "Your father seemed nice and kind though."

Lou put his arm around her and said, "My mother isn't feeling well these days. She's depressed. I'm sorry you're hurt. Please don't worry. I'm sure that she likes you."

When Millie came home she went directly to her mother's room. "Mama, I met Lou's parents and his mother hates me. Lou tried to make me feel better, but I know she does. I'll tell you what happened."

Millie told her mother about the chair with the newspapers and how Mrs. Fain ignored her, keeping herself busy. She also told her how nice Lou's father was. "Gosh Mom, I feel so bad," she said sadly.

Golda smiled, "Malkala, how could she hate you? You are a lovely girl, well-mannered, and so pretty." Golda continued. "You know sometimes people are not well and they don't mention it to anyone. In her case maybe she doesn't want to worry the family. Maybe she is afraid of losing her son. Mothers are funny sometimes with their sons. You never know. Next time you see her be your own sweet self. She'll come around. You'll see."

Millie looked at this beautiful woman, her mother. "Mom you are so bright. I am very proud to be your daughter." She put her arms around her and said, "You know so much. I hope I'll be a mother just like you." She kissed her and bid her good night.

Golda didn't go to sleep for quite a while, thinking about what her daughter told her about this young man and his family. How serious was this between her daughter and this Lou? She wondered. And why indeed did his mother act in such an unfriendly manner towards her sweet Millie? Golda loved her children. Their hurt was her hurt; their joy was her joy. She sighed deeply. Well, she told herself, with G-d's help it will work out, and she prepared for bed.

****

The family continued to grow larger. "Pina, we are blessed with such beautiful grandchildren," Golda would say gaily.

"Thank the good Lord," Pincas would always respond. "Yes Golda, all are healthy, not one wears glasses. That's because I led such a pure life."

Claire's little girl, Elaine, was eighteen months old when she thought she was pregnant again. She was frantic. "Mom, what should I do?" she cried.

Golda said, "Thank G-d for this blessing and have a healthy baby."

Claire decided to go to Dr. Miriam. When she told him her problem, he looked at her sternly and said, "Young lady, first you come to me crying because you can't become pregnant. Now you are here because you have two children and you don't want any more. Please leave."

When she left his office, he smiled and wondered if Mrs. Meirowitz knew about this. He held her in such high esteem. What would she think to hear her daughter's complaint? Happily for Claire, it turned out to be a false alarm. She was so relieved.

****

The rest of the family was doing well and by this time Golda and Pincas had eight grandchildren already. Adolph and Jean's daughter Connie was a beautiful girl who became an excellent golfer and later won a championship in the Women's Golf Divisional at Fresh Meadow Country Club.

Harry had Martin and Hanley. Millie continued to live with them, taking care of the boys and doing the marketing, etc.

Claire and Al had two children as did Nettie and Ben. Each couple had a boy and a girl. The girls, Rona and Elaine, were beautiful and bright and were always in competition because of their mothers. Nettie and Claire would each brag about their own child much to Golda's dismay.

Big Bobby, Nettie's son, was very bright. He was handsome, tall, and an excellent basketball player. When he was older, he was given a basketball scholarship at George Washington University. Little Bobby, Claire's son, was always getting into some mischief. He too was extremely bright, but in his young years he would frequently give his teachers a great deal of trouble. Obviously, he was bored in school. He eventually became a nuclear physicist and Professor.

Henry and Jane had Sharon. Jane had lost a baby girl at birth after she had Sharon. It was such a tragedy. Golda could relate to Jane's anguish and tried to comfort her as best she could.

Joe and Ethel had no children as yet. Eventually they would have three: Eugene, Linda, and Richard.

Golda was so proud of her whole family. Her sons were gentlemen, respectful, good husbands and fathers. They were comfortable—in want of nothing. Adolph had had trouble with Jean about the business right after their marriage. But once her family came into Adolph's Place and his brothers and father opened their own business, things seemed better for him.

What pleased Golda the most was the way Harry, Henry and Joe got along. They were devoted to the Place and to each other. Harry would never buy anything for his home without buying one for each of his brothers. Some years later, Ben, Nettie's husband, joined the group and still later Louis, Millie's husband, would also work for Harry.

****

Millie and Lou were falling in love and Millie was very concerned about her responsibility for Martin and Hanley. What should she do? Lou was a pharmacist and was thinking of opening his own drug store. The store Lou had his eye on was in Brooklyn, and of course that meant they would have to live there. She wouldn't be able to continue caring for her nephews if she moved away. Harry was well aware that his sister and Lou were more than just friends and he approached Millie.

"What's going on? Are you and Lou serious? Do you love him?" he questioned her.

Millie shyly confessed that she and Lou would like to become engaged, but there were problems. She explained that Lou had his eye on a drug store in Brooklyn and she just couldn't walk out on him and the boys. Yet she knew it wasn't fair to Lou either.

Harry was very touched. "You have to live your own life Millie," he said. "Would you like him to work for me? He's a fine man and very smart. He'd be good for the business."

Millie answered that she would like it very much, but only if Lou would really be willing. He suggested that he would talk to Lou. He pointed out the hardships involved in a drug store.

Harry said, "It is a business that is open every day including Saturdays and even a half day on Sundays. If you kids want to get married, why don't you work for me? You'll like our business. You'll always make a good living and you could live with me for a while."

This all sounded perfect to Millie and she was delighted by the offer, but Lou wasn't sure. His family didn't approve, even though they admitted it was a very nice offer from Harry.

Golda was worried too. "Young people should try to carry out their dreams," she said. She liked Lou, and knew that he wanted to have that drug store and to be his own boss. She also knew what a hard life a druggist lived. The store on her corner kept such long hours. They were not making enough money to hire relief. The husband and wife were in the store all day. She would prefer an easier life for her daughter, but she wouldn't interfere or try to influence Millie or Lou.

Mr. and Mrs. Fain were away for a two-week vacation in the mountains. Lou had driven them to the hotel and now it was time to bring them home. His parents invited Millie to come along and enjoy the weekend. Millie was very pleased to be asked, and as she thanked Lou, she told him she would have to ask her Mother.

Golda didn't want to be overbearing with her daughter, but at the same time she did not want Millie to go away for the weekend with a young man even though his parents were there. She answered her daughter gently.

"I'm very proud that you asked me before you answered Lou. Malkala, it isn't that Poppa and I don't trust you or Lou; it's just not right. Why can't you go on Sunday, spend the day, and come home. Mrs. Fain will have a chance to see how dear you are, and you will discover what a fine woman she is."

"O.K Mom," Millie answered happily. "I'll tell Lou."

As usual, Golda was right. Mrs. Fain was very friendly and kind to Millie. "I'm sorry I was so rude to you when you came to our apartment," she said. "The truth is, I was not well. I went to my head doctor and he helped me. Now, I'm fine and so glad you came with Louie. I hope you understand that I did not mean to hurt you."

Millie was enormously happy. Mom was right! Oh, she is so smart, thought Millie. Mrs. Fain is a fine lady and she was cordial and gracious during the visit. She was glad that Mrs. Fain confided in her and told her what had been wrong that first visit.

Lou finally decided to work for Harry and plans for a wedding were being made. Claire made a linen shower for her sister and invited Millie's friends. Among them was her friend and neighbor Rose Halpern.

Rose went to school with Millie, and her family lived just two houses away. Ben Fain, Lou's divorced brother, came to the shower. He was really charmed by Rose. "She looks just like Judy Garland," he exclaimed. They soon began to date.

Millie and Lou had set their wedding date for June 19, 1937, at the Broadway Central Hotel. It was the same wedding as Amy's except Zadie wasn't there. He had passed away a year before, and Millie was very sad about that. A day before he died, Pincas summoned all his children to come to Zadie's home to say goodbye.

Millie came with Lou. Zadie asked her, "Is this your boy?" When she nodded her head, he took both their hands and held them for a minute. "Good," he softly said. Millie smiled back at him, but it was bittersweet, knowing he would not be at her wedding.

His death was very hard for Golda. She missed him so much. She loved him and never forgot how he changed her life. If he hadn't come to Toba that day and been so kind to her, she wouldn't have married Pincas. She wouldn't have had such a fine family, wouldn't have anything.

Rose and Ben were married shortly after Millie and Lou's wedding. They took an apartment on Ocean Parkway in Brooklyn and started their new life together. Mille was happy to know that she was responsible for their meeting.

****

"Nu, Pina, here we are, just the two of us. All of our children are married, happy, and making a living. All except Harry. How I wish he would find a good woman to marry and who would be a good mother to those darling boys."

They were sitting on the porch, their most favorite place, drinking demitasse. Pincas nodded in agreement. "Golda, I pray the good Lord will make that happen. I meant to tell you that one of Harry's customers called me while I was at the Place and said she had a lovely niece. She thinks that her niece and Harry would be very happy together. I'll speak to Harry about it. I hope he'll be interested."

"Oh Pina, I do too. He needs a wife, and the children need a mother. Millie is wonderful to them, but she and Lou have to raise their own family."

They sat quietly for a while sipping their demitasse. "Golda, can you believe we are married 44 years? In six years it will be our golden anniversary?"

Golda was silent for a moment and then she said, "Pina I don't know how the years went by so quickly. I can remember so clearly how miserable I was at Toba's and how Popa rescued me, may he rest in peace. He was such a darling man. In my wildest dreams did I ever think I would have such a happy life with you and our fine children? Almost fifty years, Pina," she reached over and took his hand, "please G-d, all should be well. We'll celebrate. You know, we never had a real wedding party. Oh my, that would be so nice."

Pincas smiled as he looked lovingly at her. What a dear woman she was. He remembered how hard she worked, how she gave of herself to her family, to her in-laws, how she managed with so little money, always cheerful, so devoted to me.

"Golda," he said patting her hand, "that's just what we'll do. I'll talk to the children when the time comes."

****

Harry was dating one of Nettie's friends. She really cared for Harry and was very pleasant and attractive, but he didn't think she was the one for his boys. They went to shows, dinners, took long walks and had a good time. They almost always invited Millie and Lou to join them, but they only went once in a while. They felt it was important for Harry and Estelle to be alone. The friendship lasted for quite a while. Harry never promised her anything. He was high-principled and always told her he was not ready to marry. Their relationship was purely friendship. She seemed to be satisfied with those terms and she was good company for Harry.

Pincas sat in his chair at the front of the Place. Anyone who entered had to see him first to state their business. Many solicitors came asking for donations. Pincas never turned anyone away no matter what color, what religion. If the cause was worthy, he gave a donation.

This day when Harry wasn't too busy, Pincas called to him. "Harry, I want to talk to you. Momma and I know this woman and her family a long time. They are fine people. She called me last week to tell me about her niece Bella. She said she was good looking, she comes from a very fine family and would be a very good person for the boys as well as a devoted wife to you. I told her I would speak to you about it."

Harry smiled, "If she has such great qualities how come her aunt has to try to marry her off? She must have a wooden leg or something has got to be wrong with her."

"What have you got to lose Harry? Call her and see for yourself" Pincas urged. "It is time you found a wife and a mother for your sons. Your mother feels the same way."

"O.K. Pop. Give me the number. Maybe I'll call her." Harry did call and made a date for dinner for Saturday evening. He asked Millie and Lou to come along, but they refused.

"It's better for both of you to be alone the first time" Millie said. "If you like each other and want to go out again we'll be happy to join you."

Harry and Belle, (she liked to be called Belle) started to date often. She liked the boys and was impressed with Harry's apartment. She was happy to be in his company. Harry was becoming serious with her, enjoying their time together. Belle was knowledgeable about Jewish traditions and very willing to maintain Harry's kosher home.

One day, she came to the apartment to see if Martin, Hanley, Harry, and Millie would go to the park with her. They spent a pleasant afternoon. Harry was delighted and invited her to dinner at his parents' home.

Golda prepared a lovely meal and everyone enjoyed a good time. They talked about the two little boys, and Belle spoke lovingly about the cute things they said and did. It was evident that she was very fond of them.

"Well, what are you waiting for Harry? You are not children." Pincas asked. Get married and have a good life," he added.

"Pina, please. Harry brought Belle here so we could all meet. They know what to do. It's not your business," Golda said gently. Then she said to Belle, "Please dear, don't take offense. He wants his son to be happy, and I guess he thinks you are right for each other."

"Oh Mrs. Meirowitz, I don't mind at all. In fact I love the idea," she answered quickly.

Pincas and Golda laughed. Harry smiled but didn't say anything. After they left, while Golda was cleaning up the kitchen, Pincas was still sitting at the table.

"Would you like some more coffee" she asked?

"Yes thank you," he replied. "Tell me Golda, what do you think about Belle?" he asked.

Golda thought for a minute then answered, "She seems like a very nice girl. She likes the children, and she seems to be crazy about Harry. That's what I think. What do you think Pina?"

"I agree with you. I just hope she means every thing she says. Harry deserves a good life. He has had enough trouble. I pray that he should be happy."

On the way home Belle was very happy. "Your parents are lovely people. They were so warm and pleasant to be with. I really had a good time. I hope they like me," she added.

"I'm sure they like you. Why wouldn't they?" Harry asked.

He was quiet for a minute and then said, "Belle, I have to tell you something." He then told her all about Adolph and Jean and the business.

When he finished, he said, "I made a promise that no one would tell me who to hire or fire. No one would butt into my business. I told my late wife the same thing I'm telling you. It was fine with her and we were very happy. I'll never let my father be hurt like that again."

Belle listened intensively and said, "Wow! That's quite a story, so sad. Are they on speaking turns now?"

"Oh yes, everything is ok now. My mom saw to that. She's a remarkable woman. Her family is the most important part of her life. She would do anything for peace and happiness between her husband and children. It took me a long time to get over it, to be able to speak to my brother and Jean. My mother helped me and now you can understand how I feel about my business."

Belle said, "I certainly can understand. Harry, I don't blame you a bit and I promise you I'll never interfere in your business."

Harry then pulled over to the curb and stopped the car. "I'm glad you said that, glad you understand. And now I'm going to take my father's advice and ask- what are we waiting for? Let's get married, O. K.?" He leaned over and kissed her.

Belle laughed, "What a proposal, but I accept."

Everyone in the family was delighted and again plans were made for a wedding. Millie and Lou rented an apartment on 18th Ave. in Brooklyn and while they were very excited, Millie was already missing Martin and Hanley. The boys couldn't understand why Aunt Millie and Uncle Lou were leaving.

"We'll see each other very often," Millie assured them. "I'll come and visit you and you'll come to our home. It will be fun."

Harry and Belle had a lovely wedding and went on a honeymoon. Shortly after their return, Millie and Lou moved into their own apartment.

Harry and Belle purchased a beautiful home in Woodmere. The boys loved it. It had a large back yard and a play house. Belle was pleased with it too and, at least for the moment, everyone was happy.

Golda loved the fact that she could visit her youngest child easily, and she visited often. Every time she came, she brought a dozen dishtowels, or a tablecloth, or something for the apartment. "You really didn't have a proper trousseau like your sisters," she would say.

"Momma, don't worry. We are fine," Millie answered. She was delighted to be living near her sisters and of course her parents. Claire and Nettie would come by to spend a few hours as would Amy, Golda and Pincas. It would be a lively time when they would all stop in together, and Millie enjoyed hosting them.

For Golda, life now was very satisfying and she was content.

****

Millie missed her time with Martin and Hanley. One day she called Belle and asked if she could come and spend some time with the boys. Lou could come home with Harry. Belle said it would be lovely to see her and Millie was delighted. When she arrived, the boys were talking so fast, trying to have all of Millie's attention.

"Be quiet. Stop it," Belle reprimanded, "Go out and play in the backyard."

"Oh, it's OK Belle, really. I love to be with them. I miss them," Millie said.

"Go on. You'll visit later," Belle said again. "I'd like to have a little visit with your aunt first." Martin and Hanley went out.

She turned to Millie and asked, "So, how is everything with you? Do you like your apartment?"

Millie began to tell her how happy she and Lou were, how helpful Lou was decorating in the apartment, how considerate he was to her. Belle listened but didn't say anything, and before too long, the boys came back in.

"Aunt Millie, please come play with us now," they said eagerly. "We want you to play with us," they commanded.

Millie smiled at them. They had been so patient. "I would love to," she told them. "You don't mind Belle, if I go out with them now?" she said as she jumped up.

"Of course not," Belle answered. "I want to see about dinner anyway."

Martin and Hanley were pleased. They showed her the playhouse and they played ball. They were laughing and having a wonderful time. Millie was so glad to be with them. All too soon, it was time to get ready for dinner.

Harry and Lou arrived. Everything seemed just fine. They sat down at the table for dinner and Belle picked up the water pitcher and started to fill the glasses. She suddenly dropped the pitcher, started to cry, and ran out of the dining room.

"What did you say to her?" Harry demanded of Millie.

Shocked and frightened, Millie stammered, "Nothing, I said nothing. She asked me about our apartment and I told her. Then I went out to play with Martin and Hanley. That is all. "

Belle returned, and said quietly, "I'm sorry." Nothing was said about it after that.

The dinner was delicious, the dinner conversation was light. Soon after the end of dinner, Millie and Lou left. On the way home Millie was very quiet. "What's the matter Millie? Did you enjoy the day with Belle and the children?"

"Oh yes. I did," she answered. "But I can't understand what happened at the dinner table. Why did Harry speak to me that way? All I did was to tell her how happy we were. I only told her because she asked me how everything was. Gosh,

I just can't get over the way Belle acted. What could be wrong?"

Lou didn't comment. They drove home quietly, not saying very much other than a few words about the weather and the traffic.

Millie was still bothered the next day. While she was visiting at her mother's house she said, "Mom, I have to tell you something that happened at Belle and Harry's house yesterday."

Millie told her the whole story about what took place in the afternoon and at dinner. "I can't understand why she dropped the pitcher of water. Why did Harry yell at me?"

Golda listened quietly and then she said, "Malkala, you were talking about your happiness, and maybe this was not such a good day for Belle with the boys or with Harry and she couldn't stand it. You never know. It's a new marriage and she has to adjust to all the responsibilities. Please dear, try to forget it. You want to be welcome to visit the boys again." Golda patted her daughter and smiled, but her eyes looked troubled. I hope Harry and Belle are happy, she thought.

****

Amy had wonderful news. She was pregnant and everyone was excited, especially Millie. She started to knit sweaters, hats and blankets. She and Amy had made a most beautiful layette of knitwear by the time the baby was born. She was called Susan Mae and she was a beautiful baby.

George and Amy had a very hard time feeding her. Susan was a very poor eater. They went to all extremes to get some food into her. George would bang a spoon on a pot. The noise would frighten the baby and she would open her mouth. Amy would then get a spoonful of food into her. It was quite a sight.

It didn't take much longer when another happy announcement came from Millie and Lou. They were going to have a baby, too. Millie's pregnancy was normal, a bit of nausea in the morning, but that's all. Lou and Millie were filled with happy anticipation, and Millie spent many hours knitting a baby layette.

Fannie Fain was in the hospital for treatment of her heart. Millie went to see her every day. She loved her mother-in-law. Fannie begged her not to come so often because she was entering her ninth month, and she knew it was a strain to board the bus and travel to see her.

Millie was five days in her ninth month when her brother-in-law Al came to see her. "Just checking up on you, Mill," he said cheerfully. The truth was she didn't look that good, and he was a bit concerned.

"Want me to take you over to Mom's?" he asked.

"No thanks Al, I'll be fine," she answered. As she leaned over the sink, she took a deep breath.

"I'll come back a little later to see how you are," Al assured her.

He was a plumber and worked in the neighborhood. He had a little green Ford truck, and whenever he had time, he would take his nieces and nephews for a ride in the truck. When Al returned, Millie was glad to see him.

"OK Al, I'm ready to go to Mom's. I don't feel so great. Thanks for coming by," she said greatly relieved not to have to be alone.

"No trouble at all. Glad to be of help," he replied.

It was February 14th, Valentines Day, and it was very cold. It had snowed and the roads were getting icy. Al helped her get into the truck and drove slowly to his mother-in-law's house. He too loved Golda and enjoyed her company. He sometimes would stop off between jobs for a cup of coffee and talk.

Golda was happy to see her daughter. As time was getting close for the baby to be born, she was secretly praying that her baby, her Millie, would have an easy delivery.

"Would you like a cup of coffee, Malkala?" she asked, looking at Millie with some concern.

"No thanks Mom. I'll just sit down next to little Susan. She's so darling," she answered, trying to sound just fine. Millie was trying to make herself feel better, but she was really having quite a bit of pain.

George was home recovering from a cold, and the family was in the dinette, sitting around the table, playing with little Susan. George noticed that

Millie seemed very uncomfortable. Every so often she doubled up in pain.

George stood up and said, "Millie. I've been timing your pains and I think you are getting ready to have the baby. Call the doctor. I'm going to take you to the hospital. "

Golda looked at her daughter. She thought Millie looked a little frightened. "Go safely, Malkala. Have a healthy baby, and be a good Mommy." She put her arms around her youngest daughter and kissed her.

As she watched her leave for the hospital, a look of happy anticipation mixed with unease crossed her face. Then she turned to baby Susan thinking, soon you will have another cousin! My oh my.

Millie gave birth to a little boy that evening. Lou was delighted to be a father. "It's your Valentine present," Millie said when he kissed her.

"Mazel tov," Pincas told his daughter the next morning. "The baby is too little to have a bris. He is only five pounds and ten ounces. Nu, what can we do? We have to wait until he's six pounds."

Millie sensed a disappointment in her father's voice but she said nothing.

Later her mother-in-law called and she said, "Millie, when you see the baby, you'll notice, please, if he has finger nails and eye lashes."

"What's going on?" she thought. "Too little, finger nails, eye lashes, gosh what's wrong?"

Aloud she said, trying not to sound alarmed, "OK Mom, I'll do it."

Millie couldn't wait for the babies to be brought up for feeding. She needed to reassure herself that there was nothing to be upset about. When they did come, her baby was not among them.

"Nurse, Nurse, do you have my baby?" she tried to sound calm.

The nurse looked at the name and room number and said briskly, "No, I do not."

Millie waited until the next batch of babies came up and again her little boy was not brought to her.

"Do you have my baby?" she asked again, this time her voice was not as strong. When the nurse told her he was not brought up, Millie became alarmed.

"What's the matter? What happened? I know something is very wrong! Too little, eye lashes, fingernails, oh my dear G-d, what happened to my poor baby"? she wailed. This more than she could stand. The floor nurse heard her crying and called the head nurse.

"Why are you crying? Your baby is too tiny to be brought up, that's all. He's fine," she tried to assure Millie. But Millie was positive that her little son was not fine and couldn't be convinced.

It didn't take long before the nurse returned with a little bundle and placed it on Millie's' bed.

"Here is your baby." She said roughly. "He's perfect. Shame on you for being so selfish." She proceeded to undress the baby as Millie was crying and laughing at the same time.

"Thank you so much. I was sure I lost him. I was sure there was something terribly wrong. Oh, I'm so happy, thank you, thank you. He's so beautiful."

The nurse put the baby back in his blanket and as she left to bring him back to the nursery she said a bit more gently, "Now rest and don't carry on anymore."

"Oh, I'm so thrilled," Millie exclaimed as she lay down in her bed. "Thank you again."

She settled herself in the bed and smiled as she dialed her mother's number.

"Hi Mom." Not waiting for her to respond she continued, "I saw the baby. He is beautiful, so darling, but so tiny. Mom, I'm scared."

"Don't be worried, Malkala. It's a big world and he'll grow up to be a strong man. What are you going to name him?"

"Lou and I decided to name him after Zaida. We'll call him Stephen Michael," answered Millie.

"Oh that's a beautiful name. Shloma Meyer in Hebrew."

Golda was so happy that her father-in-law had a name. Susan was named for him too, but this baby had the same Hebrew name. Oh how she had loved that man, of blessed memory.

"It's a beautiful name," she said again to Millie. "I'll say goodbye darling. Get some rest. Be a healthy mother."

"I want to be a mom just like you," Millie said.

"Thank you, Malkala." She hung up the phone and went into her bright cheery kitchen.

****

Amy was sitting at the table feeding Susan her bottle. Golda stood in the doorway watching. What a lovely picture. How lovingly and gently Amy handled her baby. Her memory took her back to when her children were babies and she fed them. The only difference was she didn't use bottles. She had nursed her children for two years. It was a birth control method as well as an intimate and loving activity.

Amy worked hard in the house. She was immaculate. Golda was not able to do the things she used to do and Amy spared her.

"Mom, sit down. I'll take care of it," Amy would say if Golda tried to do a chore. It was wonderful for Golda to have Amy live with them. However, Golda was bothered because she had a feeling that George and Amy would like to be in their own place.

"Pina, I want to talk to you about Amy and George. I think they would like to live alone but are not saying anything because they don't want to hurt us. Pina, remember how we loved our first little home? It wasn't much at all, but we were so happy."

"Yes Golda, I remember, and if you think they want to move out, I wouldn't blame them at all. But Golda could you manage without Amy?"

"Pina that is not the issue. Don't you think she and George are entitled to have their own place? Of course I'll miss her. But I'll manage. I'm going to speak to her."

Golda waited until lunch was over and Amy was sitting outside with Susan who was sleeping in her carriage. She came out and sat down next to Amy. "It's a lovely day," she said.

"Yes it is, Mom. Is everything all right? You look a little worried."

"I'm not exactly worried. A little concerned. Amy honey, you are so dear to Poppa and me, and you work so hard. I have a feeling that you and George would really like to be in your own home. I want you to know how much we appreciate what you and George both do for us, and that being with Susan is a joy. At the same, time you should have what you want."

Amy was listening to her Mother. "Mom, you and Poppa are so sweet and whatever we do for you is a pleasure. I will admit we have talked about getting our own place, but the thought of leaving you frightens me. Of course if we do, it will not be far away. We'll see," Amy said as she leaned over to kiss her mother.

Amy and George did find a house near her parents. Amy visited every day, cleaning the bathroom and kitchen over Golda's protests. "You don't have to do this Amy dear. I can do it myself."

"Mom, it takes no time and I'm happy to help you a little," Amy replied. They spent a good part of the day together playing with Susan, having lunch and visiting with Claire, Nettie, Millie, and the other grandchildren.

****

The family was still growing. Golda and Pincas were great-grand parents. Connie and Jerry were so happy with their daughter, Susan. Amy and George were the happy parents of a second child, a little boy whom they called Buzzy. His name was Irwin Leslie, but Amy liked the name of Buzzy.

Golda was pleased that the family was getting together once a month for a family circle. These get-togethers were at a different home every month. The hostess always served a lovely dinner. The evening was enjoyable to all especially to Golda. She loved her family dearly and they in turn loved her.

Harry called her almost everyday from the Place. "Mom, how are you? Is everything alright? Do you need anything?"

"Hershala, everything is fine. Thank you so much," she would assure him. And she would smile contentedly.

****

Mille and Lou wanted a larger apartment as they were hoping to have another child. They found a nice two bedroom in a duplex on East 7th Street on the ground floor.

Stevie was a darling boy—bright, cheerful and happy to share whatever he had with the neighborhood children. On rainy days, Millie would invite the children from the block to come in and she would show movies and serve treats. The children loved to go to Stevie's home and Stevie was happy to have them.

Millie soon became pregnant and had a beautiful little girl. Fannie Fain named her Devorah Basha after her mother, and Millie and Lou named her Dianne Barbara. She weighed seven pounds and two ounces and was a healthy darling baby. Millie and Lou were delighted.

"Now, we have a perfect family," Milllie said happily to Lou.

****

Harry's business was good, but the world situation was unpredictable, and buying fabric was becoming costly. It was hard to get the plaid taffeta in quantity. He talked to the boys and they agreed to buy a mill that would service only them. It would be a very lucrative move.

Harry found a mill that was for sale in Patterson, New Jersey. He offered to buy it and put Lou in business. Lou would make the patterns and run the whole mill. Gradually, he would pay it off to Harry.

Lou was very bright and easily figured out how to count the threads and make beautiful plaid patterns. The only hardship was the traveling. He drove from Brooklyn to Patterson everyday and many times he was so tired and sleepy that he would pull off the road and take a nap. He thought about moving, but he knew how happy Millie was to be near his and her family.

Millie was well aware of his travel hardship, and she spoke to her Mother. "Mom," she said, "Lou and I will have to find a house in New Jersey, not too far from the mill. I know I'll miss all of you so much, especially Amy. But what can I do?"

Golda looked at her daughter and smiled. "I'm so proud of you Millie. You are absolutely right. A wife goes where her husband's penusa (*job*) takes them. G-D forbid, he could have an accident driving so far. Don't worry; we'll visit you."

Belle was familiar with New Jersey and advised Lou to look for a house in Caldwell. She told him it is known as the Denver of the east and is only fifteen minutes from Patterson. There were no factories in Caldwell, in fact, the air is so pure that Teressa Gratta, a well known hospital for people with respiratory ailments, is located there.

Lou went to Caldwell and found a most suitable house. He brought Millie to see it. She loved the charming colonial home on Kramer Avenue. They bought the house and enjoyed living there for many years.

****

America was at war with Germany. Men and women volunteered to serve in the military and men were being drafted into the army. Ben, Joe, George, and Lou received draft notices at the time of the first Passover Seder.

Ben was declared 4-F because he had a hernia. That meant he would be in the service, but would not be called to active duty. He would most likely be given a desk job. Joe wasn't classified as yet because they thought he might have high blood pressure. Lou was classified 1-A which made him eligible for active duty. That was a real surprise because he had a herniated disk and everyone was so sure that her would be rejected.

The Seder is usually a most happy time, but this evening was very quiet. The sisters were going about the serving and clearing without a smile, just tending to the needs of the family.

"What's wrong?" Pincas asked. "I brought up the best wine. It's number one. Why aren't you singing the way we always do on Pesach?"

Nobody answered. They had decided not to tell the folks because they would worry.

The next day there was an announcement on the radio news and in the newspaper that men who had a family and were over 30 years of age were exempt from military service. There was such happiness and exuberance at the second Seder. Everyone sang to Pincas' delight.

"Golda," Pincas said, "it is so wonderful to have all our children and grandchildren at our table. Look how beautiful they are."

"Yes, I know Pina. But the poor Jews in Germany and Poland and other European countries are suffering so. I can't stop thinking that if you weren't called to America to perform the ceremony of Halitza, we would be the same. Victims. Oh Pina, what can be done? What can we do?"

"Golda, we must pray for them and have faith in America."

Sidney Fain, Lou's youngest brother, had volunteered to serve in the army. He was to leave for England and Fannie, Elias, Millie and Lou went to see him off. It was a bleak day and the mood of all the people on the pier matched the weather. Fannie stood waving a small American flag, tears flowing down her cheeks as the ship sailed out of sight.

"G-d bless them and keep them safe," she said softly.

1944

One evening when Pincas was preparing for bed he called to Golda, "Golda, I have something to tell you."

Golda came into their bedroom and sat down on her bed. "What's the news? Oh I do hope it's good."

"Oh, it's good, Goldala. You'll be very happy. Harry is going to call Claire to start planning our

50th wedding celebration. It's next year, can you believe it? And there is so much to celebrate."

"Oh Pina, I'm so excited. Please G-d everyone should be well. We never had a wedding celebration; can you imagine? Oh this will be wonderful," she exclaimed.

"I knew that would make you happy. I don't know what he plans to do, but I'm sure whatever it is, it will be in good taste."

About two weeks later, Harry called his sister on the phone. "Claire, I want you to contact the East Midwood Jewish Center and reserve the date for Mom and Poppa's 50th wedding anniversary. I want them to have a beautiful party. Everyone will be invited, all our relatives, in-laws, everybody they know and like. Don't worry about the cost. I'll take care of everything."

"O.K. Harry," Claire said happily. "I'll take care of it."

Claire made the reservation eight months in advance. The time passed quickly and before Golda knew it, she was being fitted for a dress. It was black lace with a gold thread through it, just gorgeous. A fabulous menu was ordered. Everything was done in gold. There were to be yellow roses all around the room, white tablecloths and gold napkins. Golda was in a sort of trance.

She was so happy and in awe of the preparations. Pina enjoyed watching her. All the in-law family was invited, all the friends from Europe who had come to America, all the friends they had made over the years. Golda and Pinas' eight children and their mates were beautifully dressed. The women wore orchids; the men wore boutonnieres.

They had a lovely ceremony. The children and grandchildren led the procession. Pincas walked down the aisle and then sat down under the chupa (*wedding canopy*). Golda walked down with Harry, they both were beaming with happiness.

As they walked down, someone said, "That's his Mom."

Harry heard that and he put his arms around Golda and lifted her up and said, "You bet she is."

The ceremony was over and then the real party began. There was music and much dancing. Henry dancing with his daughter Sharon was a lovely sight. They played horahs and Golda joined the circle. She was dancing when Harry stopped her.

"Mom, please don't. I don't want you to overdo. Remember you had that mini-stroke. Come sit down." He walked her to her table and she gave him a little kiss as she sat down.

Ethel and Joe's little girl Linda was about five years old and was a marvelous piano player. She played by ear. Ethel wanted her to have piano lessons, but teachers advised her not to start her yet. She played at the party and everyone was just amazed. She really was wonderful and Golda and Pincas were so proud.

It was a night to remember and Golda and Pincas never forgot it. They were very proud of their family and so happy to share their simcha with all the people who attended the party. So many presents were received that their dining table was laden with gifts. Golda would open some every day. It was her way of making the joy of her party last longer.

****

Six months later, Golda suffered a cerebral hemorrhage. She was taken to The Brooklyn Jewish Hospital. During that time her children and Pincas visited her very often. Pincas was very quiet. His pain and loneliness was unmistakable.

During one visit, Millie noticed a beautiful vase of eighteen yellow roses on the windowsill. She read the card aloud. It said, Chi Stim Laben (*to a long life*), signed Jeanne, Adolph, and Connie.

"Oh Momma, how beautiful."

Golda smiled and put her arms as if she was holding a baby.

"Mom, is Connie pregnant?" Golda nodded. "Mom, I'm pregnant, too."

Golda put her hand to her heart and looked up as if to say thank G-d. The private nurse asked Millie to stay with her while she went out to get some papers.

"Don't give her anything. No water; nothing. She could choke," the nurse warned.

No sooner did the nurse leave, then Golda in much labored speech said, "ah leffel vasser" (a *spoonful of water*).

Millie panicked. She remembered what the nurse had said. Millie went to the door and looked out. She saw the nurse coming down the corridor.

"Hurry!" she whispered urgently. "My Mom needs you."

The nurse came in quickly. When she saw Golda, she immediately made a call for assistance. She then asked Millie to leave the room.

"What's happening? Oh my G-d," cried Millie. "I should have given her a sip of water."

"No, no my dear," answered the nurse. "You did just right, but now you must step out of the room so that we can try to help you mother." Just then, a doctor and another nurse entered the room and closed the door.

When the door finally opened, Golda was quiet. A balloon was attached to her mouth and she appeared to be sleeping.

"Is she going to be OK?" asked the tearful Millie.

"We hope so," the nurse answered. "Go home now and take a rest. You will need all your strength. The family will be here."

"I guess you're right," Millie reluctantly answered and left for home. She returned the next day and found Harry there. When the doctor came in to check on Golda, Harry approached him.

"Doctor," he said, "she's getting better isn't she?" he said expectantly. It was sad to see this man, Harry, who was not very tall, standing in front of the tall doctor, looking up with hope in his face.

"She can't get better, Harry," the doctor said. "I told you. She has what President Roosevelt had: a cerebral hemorrhage. I'm so sorry."

"But Doctor," Harry said. "You'll make her well."

The doctor didn't answer. He just patted Harry and said again, "I'm sorry."

Golda died that Saturday, just 10 days after she was admitted into the hospital, and the family prepared for the funeral.

"We'll have it at the Riverside Chapel in Manhattan and then proceed to our shul," Harry suggested to Adolph, who nodded in agreement. Our Rabbi Goldstein will officiate.

"Harry," Millie asked, "do you think we should have it in Brooklyn in Papa and Mamma's shul? She fed all those men on Shabbos, and in the Sukkah, and you know, Harry, Papa was Gabba there. H e was the one who gave out the honors."

"No, Millie," Harry replied. "But I'll have a limousine or two for whoever wants to come from that shul."

The chapel was filled with family, friends, and business associates. Golda was not viewed, but before the service, the family was able to see her. She looked beautiful. She had a lace head covering which came to the bridge of her nose.

She looked like she was sleeping peacefully. Then it was time to close the coffin and wheel it into the chapel.

The Rabbi started to speak. "My dear friends, I did not have the privilege of knowing Golda Meirowitz, but she must have been a golden woman to have sons like Harry and Adolph. The Rabbi proceeded to praise them and mention the various contributions to United Jewish Appeal, Israel, Jewish National Fund and other community projects.

Suddenly there was a stirring in the room. Pincas was rising up from his seat with some difficulty. He stood up and slowly made his way to the front of the room and stood near the coffin. The room was deafeningly quiet and the Rabbi said nothing.

Pincas placed his hand on the coffin and said, "Minea tiera frient (*my dear friends*), I would like to tell you that my wife was a true Ayshis Chayel

(*Woman of Valor*),a true good soul, a wonderful wife, mother, grandmother and friend. She fed anyone who came to her hungry. She would leave a saucer of milk out her back door just in case a dog or cat wandered by. She was a true daughter of Israel."

He touched the coffin again and slowly walked back to his seat.

The family tearfully recited the Kadish together, Rabbi Goldstein sang the El Moleh Rachamin, and the service ended. The coffin, followed by the family, left the chapel.

The hearse, followed by the funeral procession consisting of many limousines and cars, stopped at Golda and Pinicas' synagogue. The doors of the hearse and of the shul were opened as were the doors on the bima (*the place where the Torahs are kept*). The Rabbi chanted a Hebrew prayer.

Then the hearse slowly proceeded on and turned into Mount Zion Cemetery. They slowed down at the first Romanian Synagogue area and came to a stop at block 38. It was a closed off area, with the name Meirowitz on it.

There were sixteen gravesites within the area, two of which were already taken; one was Hannah, Harry's first wife, who died on July 15, 1932 and the other was Baby Meirowitz, Henry and Jane's newborn child, who died in 1939.

As family and friends took turns covering her coffin with a blanket of earth, there was a respectful silence. Although this woman was not tall in stature, she was a giant in raising her eight children and instilling in them character, honesty, and love for humankind. Each person remembered the special moments they had with her. They left slowly and silently, drifting back to their cars. Pincas was the last.

Rest in peace, Golda Meirowitz, Ayshis Chayel.

****